british food

photography by Jason Lowe

quadrille

This edition first published in 2005 by **Quadrille Publishing Limited**
Alhambra House, 27-31 Charing Cross Road, London WC2H 0LS

Editorial director Jane O'Shea
Creative director Helen Lewis
Managing editor Janet Illsley
Art direction Vanessa Courtier
Editor Lewis Esson
Design Ros Holder and Claire Peters
Photographer Jason Lowe
Food stylists Mark Hix and Stuart Gillies
Props stylist Jane Campsie
Production Ruth Deary

Text © 2003 Mark Hix **Photography** © 2003 Jason Lowe
Design and layout © 2005 Quadrille Publishing Limited

Originally published exclusively for J Sainsbury plc.

Cataloguing in Publication Data: a catalogue record for this book is available
from the British Library.

ISBN 1 84400 213 6
Printed in China

Cookery notes
All spoon measures are level: 1 tsp = 5ml spoon; 1 tbsp = 15ml spoon.
Use fresh herbs and freshly ground black pepper unless otherwise suggested.
Free-range eggs are recommended and large eggs should be used except
where a different size is specified. Recipes with raw or lightly cooked eggs
should be avoided by anyone who is pregnant or in a vulnerable health group.

Contents

Introduction

Over the last two decades, we have rediscovered the pleasures of eating and cooking in this country. In general, we have become more knowledgeable about all sorts of food – thanks to food writers, TV chefs, supermarkets and specialist food stores, regular foreign holidays and adventurous new restaurants. Until recently, at least, this revolution has largely been based on foreign cuisines and newly imported ingredients from afar. Many of our own traditional fruits and vegetables, rare breeds of cattle and poultry, and artisan food products like cheeses and hams have been overlooked. Now, fortunately, our finest indigenous foods are being revived and reintroduced into our diets, in the wake of our rediscovery of cooking in general.

Old-fashioned vegetables that fell out of our ken, like Jerusalem artichokes and sea kale, are reappearing in our shops. Forgotten varieties of fruits, like quince, and rare types of apples are being marketed anew. Restaurants are also using tastier, less expensive cuts of meat, once designated as poor man's food. Hocks, shins, shanks and necks are now common on most restaurant menus in some form or another, and this gives people the confidence to buy these cuts from the butcher and recreate tasty dishes at home.

Many British puddings have an interesting history of some kind, often linked to royalty or other famous old households or institutions, conjuring up images of grand kitchens in full swing, preparing dishes that we've almost forgotten. British puddings have a reputation for being stodgy, but given a fresh approach they can be full of flavour and still comforting. And what could be better than serving them with some thick Jersey or clotted cream?

People are again waking up to the fact that there is a British cuisine that we can not only be proud of, but one that we can relish, explore and develop. I often come across an old dish that I've either forgotten about or never heard of in the first place, and can't wait to get it on the menu. Where appropriate, I'll give it a fresh modern twist to bring it up to date. This is the approach I have taken with the recipes in this book, as some of the ingredients I value for their flavour today were not widely available in Britain when these dishes where originally created. The passion for British food is gradually creeping back into our homes and on to our tables. In writing this book, my aim is to help you in this exciting process of rediscovery.

Guide to ingredients

In Britain we are actually blessed with some of the finest ingredients in the world, although lots of them don't always find their way into our normal shopping territory and we may have to go searching for them. Nowadays, hough, there aren't many ingredients we can't get our hands on if we try, thanks to farmers' markets, specialist suppliers and supermarkets becoming increasingly adventurous.

We may take for granted certain indigenous foods that stare us in the face daily. For example, Scotland has an international reputation for some of the finest beef in the world, some of our best wild mushrooms come from the Highlands, and Scottish seafood, like oysters, scallops and langoustines (Dublin Bay prawns), are prized and exported all over the world. Oysters are a part of English history. The Romans loved our Colchester oysters so much they designated the town, Camulodunum as it was then called, the capital of Roman England. Except for oyster enthusiasts who tend to take them for granted, most of us miss out on their pure taste of the sea.

We rarely put things into our shopping trolley unless we've tried them before and enjoyed them. We all know what to do with most of our common ingredients but rarely deviate into experimentation, even if it's a simple concoction like colcannon (page 217), or flavouring our mash with mustard to go with sausages. Vegetables like celeriac and Jerusalem artichokes often sit on the shelves until they have passed their sell-by dates because few of us know how to tackle their knobbly exteriors.

If, like me, you enjoy living off the land, you can enjoy your own wild mushrooms when in season, as well as things like samphire and other sea vegetables like sea beet. Obviously, when it comes to wild mushrooms, you need to know what you are picking and you should only do so if you can differentiate between edible and non-edible varieties with total confidence.

Gathering food from the wild makes you appreciate the seasons for what they are and you also come to understand how our weather can affect the growth of produce so much. These days, sadly, you rarely see families armed with baskets picking wild blackberries and other soft fruits in the woods; if you do get the chance, though, take the kids for a walk with the basket, show them how food really grows and get them to pick their own supper.

Whenever I hear the phrase 'in season', I automatically take more interest, as it's a joy to be offered something on the menu that uses a native ingredient in its prime. In our restaurants we keep our menus as seasonal as possible to make life interesting for both our customers and chefs. When you get customers asking when the elvers or gull's eggs are starting, you know you are sending out that seasonal message on the menu. Although nowadays most ingredients are available all year round, flown in from some part of the world or another, food in season in your own neck of the woods usually has more flavour and is certainly almost always cheaper.

Tender green asparagus is one of the classic English vegetables and I just can't wait for May to come when home-grown asparagus will be with us for 4–6 weeks, depending on how temperamental the weather is. It's the same for most of our fruit and vegetables – the seasons can be as long or short as the weather allows them, but even so we have amazing ingredients throughout the year.

The arrival of the first Jersey Royal potatoes informs us that spring is here and it's going to get warmer, hopefully. Apart from asparagus, don't miss out on the pick of the other early summer vegetables – young, tender broad beans and sweet, tender peas in particular. Summer salad leaves have certainly moved on since the days of the floppy English round lettuce. Forgotten salad leaf varieties have been revived and vegetable leaves like spinach and chard are harvested in their juvenile stage for the salad bowl. The good old English strawberry is, of course, symbolic of midsummer, with Wimbledon and sunshine.

With our increasing awareness of our food heritage, we are once again enthusiastically marking the passage of the year by anticipating the arrival of seasonal produce ... fresh spring lamb, lush summer berries, autumnal game birds, chestnuts and wild mushrooms, and the root vegetables and Brussels sprouts of winter. There is also a natural synergy of ingredients, in that foods in season at the same time usually work particularly well together, like lamb and broad beans, or apples and blackberries.

Seasonal availability of ingredients

To help you make the most of our seasonal produce, I have listed British ingredients in the months in which I find they are at their best to eat.

January: sprats, Cornish cauliflower, forced rhubarb

February: purple sprouting broccoli, spring shallot shoots, Brussels sprouts, celeriac, leeks

March: new-season's garlic, garlic shoots, nettles, sea kale

April: elvers, razor clams, guinea fowl and pheasant eggs, Jersey Royal potatoes, St George's mushrooms, wild sorrel

May: crabs, gull's eggs, asparagus, peas, broad beans, watercress

June: wild salmon, sea trout, new-season's carrots, sprouting broccoli, radishes, sea beet, wild fennel, horseradish, cultivated strawberries, Discovery apples, chamomile, elderflowers

July: samphire, sweetcorn, tomatoes, runner beans, lettuce, gooseberries, strawberries, raspberries, cherries, purslane, thyme

August: cucumbers, Scottish girolles, gooseberries, pears, wild strawberries, blackcurrants, Dorset blueberries, tayberries, loganberries, sloes

September: beetroot, chard, pumpkins, ceps, pears, field mushrooms, crab apples, elderberries, blackberries

October: native oysters, mussels, turbot, chanterelles, oyster mushrooms, puff balls, Cox's orange pippins, hazelnuts, chestnuts, rowanberries, Kentish cob nuts, walnuts

November: parsnips, swede, Jerusalem artichokes

December: goose, quince

Seasonal availability of game birds

Grouse: August 12 – December 10
Snipe: August 12 – January 31
Partridge: September 1 – February 1
Mallard: September 1 – February 20
Pheasant: October 1 – February 1

british stocks and soups

Vegetable stock

Makes 1–1.5 litres (1¾–2½ pints)
3 onions, peeled and roughly
 chopped
3 garlic cloves, peeled and roughly
 chopped
1 small head of celery, roughly
 chopped
3 leeks, well rinsed and roughly
 chopped

5 carrots, peeled and roughly
 chopped
2 bay leaves
few thyme sprigs
20 black peppercorns
small bunch of parsley
1 tsp fennel seeds

1 Place all the ingredients in a large saucepan and add cold water to cover.
Bring to the boil, skim and simmer for 30–40 minutes.
2 Strain the liquor through a fine sieve. Taste and if the flavour isn't strong
enough, boil to reduce the stock down.

A well flavoured stock makes all the difference
– to soups and sauces in particular. You can
either buy good quality fresh stock or make
your own. Don't add salt to your stock, as you
may want to reduce it down later.

Dark meat stock

Also illustrated on following page

Makes 1–1.5 litres (1¾–2½ pints)
2kg (4½lb) chopped beef, veal, lamb
    or chicken bones, or a mixture
3 onions, peeled for a lighter stock
    and roughly chopped
5 carrots, peeled and roughly
    chopped
few celery stalks, roughly chopped

2 leeks, well rinsed and roughly
    chopped
½ head of garlic
1½ tbsp tomato purée
10 black peppercorns
few thyme sprigs
1 bay leaf

1 Preheat the oven to 200°C (fan oven 180°C), gas mark 6. Put the chopped meat bones in a roasting tin with the vegetables and garlic and roast for about 15–20 minutes until golden brown, stirring every so often. Stir in the tomato purée and roast for another 10 minutes.
2 Tip the bones and vegetables into a large saucepan, cover with cold water and add the black peppercorns, thyme sprigs and bay leaf. Bring to the boil, skim and simmer for 3–4 hours, skimming occasionally and topping up with water as necessary to keep the ingredients covered.
3 Strain through a fine sieve, then skim off any fat. Taste and, if the flavour isn't strong enough, boil to reduce down and concentrate.

Note If making a sauce, reduce the stock until starting to thicken and add a little cornflour mixed with water to achieve the consistency required.

Raw bones make a better stock than leftover cooked ones, so ask your butcher to keep some for you – they'll need to be chopped up.

Chicken stock

Makes 1–1.5 litres (1¾–2½ pints)

2kg (4½lb) chicken bones, rinsed and chopped

3 leeks, well rinsed and roughly chopped

3 onions, peeled for a lighter stock and roughly chopped

3 celery stalks, roughly chopped

1 bay leaf

few thyme sprigs

2 garlic cloves, peeled and chopped

10 black peppercorns

1 Place all the ingredients in a large saucepan and add cold water to cover. Bring to the boil, skim and simmer for 2 hours, topping up with water and skimming as necessary.

2 Strain the liquor through a fine sieve. Taste and if the flavour isn't strong enough, boil to reduce the stock down.

When you make stock, do so in quantity, then boil down to concentrate and freeze in useful quantities. To darken the colour of the stock, if required, leave the skin on the onions.

Fish stock

Illustrated on page 23

Makes 1–1.5 litres (1¾–2½ pints)
2kg (4½lb) white fish bones (sole,
  brill, etc), rinsed
2 leeks, well rinsed and roughly
  chopped
2 onions, peeled and roughly
  chopped

½ head of celery, roughly chopped
½ lemon
1 tsp fennel seeds
20 black peppercorns
1 bay leaf
few thyme sprigs
handful of parsley

1 Place all the ingredients in a large saucepan and add cold water to cover.
Bring to the boil and skim, then lower the heat and simmer gently for
20 minutes, skimming occasionally.
2 Strain the liquor through a fine sieve. Taste the stock and boil to reduce if
the flavour isn't strong enough.

Don't overcook this stock or it will lose its
freshness and may have a bitter taste.

Jerusalem artichoke and rosemary soup

Serves 4–6

good knob of butter

1 small onion, peeled and roughly chopped

1 small leek, trimmed, roughly chopped and rinsed

few rosemary sprigs

500g (1lb 2oz) Jerusalem artichokes, peeled

750ml (1¼ pints) vegetable stock

750ml (1¼ pints) milk

2 tbsp double cream

sea salt and white pepper

1 Melt the butter in a saucepan, add the onion, leek and rosemary sprigs, and cook gently for about 10 minutes until the vegetables are soft. Add the Jerusalem artichokes, most of the vegetable stock and the milk, and lightly season with salt and pepper. Bring to the boil, lower the heat and simmer for about 25 minutes until the artichokes are tender.

2 Whiz the soup in a blender or using a hand-held stick blender until smooth, adding the reserved stock if necessary, to adjust the consistency. Pass through a fine-meshed sieve into a clean pan.

3 Add the cream to the soup and reheat gently to just below the boil, stirring. Adjust the seasoning if necessary before serving.

The Jerusalem artichoke has a lovely nutty, earthy flavour and makes an excellent soup. Use a free-standing or hand-held stick blender to purée soups, rather than a food processor, which won't give a comparable velvety texture.

Creamed onion soup with cider

Serves 4–6

1 tbsp vegetable oil
5 medium onions, peeled and thinly
   sliced
1 tsp chopped thyme leaves
good knob of butter

1 tbsp plain flour
125ml (4fl oz) dry cider
1 litre (1¾ pints) vegetable stock
2 tbsp double cream
sea salt and pepper

1 Heat the oil in a heavy-based pan, then add the sliced onions and thyme. Cover and cook gently for about 10 minutes until the onions are soft but not coloured.

2 Add the butter and allow to melt, then sprinkle in the flour and stir over a low heat for a minute or so. Slowly add the cider, stirring constantly, then gradually add the vegetable stock and season with salt and pepper. Bring to the boil and simmer for 45 minutes.

3 Stir in the cream and check the seasoning. Ladle into warm soup plates and serve.

Here is the British answer to classic French onion soup. The addition of cider sweetens the onions and gives the soup a mellow flavour, quite unlike its French counterpart.

Watercress soup with goat's cheese

Illustrated on previous pages

Serves 4–6

250g (9oz) watercress, washed

1 tbsp vegetable or corn oil

1 leek, trimmed, roughly chopped
and rinsed

1 small floury potato, about 75–100g
(3–3½oz), peeled and diced

1.2 litres (2 pints) vegetable stock

100g (3½oz) fresh soft English goat's
cheese

sea salt and pepper

1 Cut the main stalks from the watercress and reserve. Heat the oil in a pan, add the leek and potato, cover and cook gently for about 10 minutes until soft, without allowing them to colour. Add the vegetable stock, season with salt and pepper and bring to the boil. Simmer for 10 minutes, then add the watercress stalks and simmer for another 5 minutes.

2 Remove from the heat and add the watercress sprigs. Whiz the soup in a blender or using a hand-held stick blender until smooth, then pass through a fine-meshed sieve into a clean pan. If serving hot, reheat the soup briefly and season again with salt and pepper, if necessary. If serving cold, cool, then chill and check the seasoning before serving.

3 Pour the watercress soup into bowls and top each portion with a spoonful of soft goat's cheese. Serve at once.

This fresh-tasting soup is a great way to appreciate the taste of watercress. Brief cooking and quick chilling are essential to preserve the delicate flavour.

Cullen skink

Illustrated on previous pages

Serves 4–6
1 leek, trimmed
good knob of butter
1.2 litres (2 pints) fish stock
1 floury potato, about 200g (7oz),
    peeled and roughly chopped
1 bay leaf
300g (11oz) undyed smoked haddock
    fillets
4 tbsp double cream
1 tbsp chopped parsley
sea salt and white pepper

1 Roughly chop the leek and rinse thoroughly in cold water, then drain and pat dry. Melt the butter in a pan, stir in the leek, cover and cook gently for a few minutes until soft.
2 Add the fish stock, potato, bay leaf and smoked haddock. Bring to a simmer, season and cook gently for 15 minutes. With a slotted spoon, carefully remove the smoked haddock from the pan to a plate and put to one side. Simmer the soup for a further 15 minutes.
3 Remove the bay leaf and whiz the soup in a blender or using a hand-held stick blender until it is smooth. Pass through a fine-meshed sieve into a clean pan.
4 Skin and flake the smoked haddock, checking for any bones. Stir the cream and parsley into the soup and bring back to a simmer. Add the flaked haddock and adjust the seasoning, if necessary. Heat through gently, then serve in warm soup plates.

Cullen is the village on the coast of the Moray Firth where this classic Scottish soup came from, and 'skink' is an ancient word for a broth or soup. This soup is substantial enough to be served as a main course or brunch dish.

Cornish red mullet soup

Serves 4–6

2 tbsp olive oil

500g (1lb 2oz) whole red mullet, cleaned and roughly chopped

1 small onion, peeled and roughly chopped

½ leek, trimmed, roughly chopped and rinsed

½ small fennel bulb, roughly chopped

½ red pepper, deseeded and roughly chopped

1 small potato, about 125g (4oz), peeled and roughly chopped

3 garlic cloves, peeled and chopped

good pinch of saffron threads

5 black peppercorns

2 juniper berries

1 bay leaf

few thyme sprigs

3 tbsp tomato purée

150g canned chopped tomatoes

150ml (¼ pint) red wine

1.5 litres (2½ pints) fish stock

sea salt and pepper

1 Heat the olive oil in a large heavy-based pan and gently fry the chopped red mullet, vegetables, garlic, spices and herbs for about 10 minutes. Add the tomato purée, chopped tomatoes, red wine and fish stock. Bring to the boil, season with salt and pepper, and simmer for 50 minutes.

2 Blend about one third of the soup (bones and all) in a blender or using a hand-held stick blender until smooth. Return to the rest of the soup in the pan and simmer gently for another 20 minutes.

3 Strain the soup by pushing it through a medium-meshed sieve or conical strainer with the back of a ladle into a clean pan. Reheat gently and adjust the seasoning to serve.

British red mullet is seasonal and can be hard to find, but you could use sea bream, sea bass or gurnard, or even a mixture of fish. The soup freezes well, so consider making a double batch when you come across fresh red mullet.

Leek and oyster soup

Serves 4

good knob of butter

3 medium leeks, trimmed, roughly
   chopped and rinsed

750ml (1¼ pints) fish stock

8 oysters, opened (see page 64),
   juices saved

2 tbsp double cream

1 tbsp finely chopped chives

sea salt and white pepper

1 Melt the butter in a pan, add the leeks, cover and cook gently until soft, without allowing them to colour. Add the fish stock, bring to the boil, season with salt and pepper and simmer for 10 minutes.

2 Remove from the heat and add half of the oysters and the cream. Whiz the soup in a blender or using a hand-held stick blender until smooth.

3 Pass the soup through a fine-meshed sieve into a clean pan and season again, if necessary. Bring back to a simmer, then remove from the heat and add the remaining oysters and the chives.

4 Serve in warm shallow soup bowls or pasta bowls, spooning an oyster into each one.

For those of you who are squeamish about oysters, this soup is a great introduction to these little gems. The flavour of the sea is still present, but the oysters are no longer alive.

Crab soup

Illustrated on previous pages

Serves 4–6

1kg (2¼lb) prepared whole crab
  (see page 68)
1 tbsp vegetable oil
1 small onion, peeled and roughly
  chopped
1 small leek, trimmed, chopped and
  rinsed
3 garlic cloves, peeled and roughly
  chopped

½ tsp fennel seeds
few thyme sprigs
1 bay leaf
40g (1½oz) butter
2 tbsp tomato purée
3 tbsp flour
1 glass of dry white wine
1.5 litres (2½ pints) fish stock
100ml (3½fl oz) double cream
sea salt and white pepper

1 Set the crabmeat to one side. With a heavy chopping knife or cleaver, break the body and leg shells up into small pieces. Heat the oil in a large heavy-based saucepan and fry the crab shells over a high heat for about 5 minutes, stirring every so often until they begin to colour.

2 Add the onion, leek, garlic, fennel seeds, thyme and bay leaf, and cook for another 5 minutes or until the vegetables begin to colour. Add the butter and melt, then add the tomato purée and flour, stir well and cook gently for a minute or so. Add the wine, then slowly stir in the fish stock. Bring to the boil, lower the heat, season and simmer for 1 hour.

3 Strain the soup through a colander over a bowl. Discard the hard claws and main shell, retaining about one third of the softer white body shells in the colander. Add these to the strained liquid and whiz in a blender or strong food processor, then strain through a fine-meshed sieve into a clean pan.

4 Bring the soup to a simmer, then stir in the cream and crabmeat. Warm through gently, check the seasoning and serve in warm bowls.

This soup acquires its flavour from the shells of the crab, so you can use most of the meat for a salad or sandwich. If you can't get whole crabs, use cooked or raw prawns in shells with heads instead.

Scotch broth

Serves 4–6

50g (2oz) dried green or yellow split
  peas
25g (1oz) pearl barley
200g (7oz) neck of lamb fillet
½ tsp chopped thyme leaves
2 litres (3½ pints) lamb or chicken
  stock
1 small leek, trimmed, slit lengthways
  and rinsed

2 carrots, peeled
1 celery stalk, strings removed if
  necessary
1 small turnip, peeled
few leaves of green cabbage, stalks
  removed
1 tbsp chopped parsley
sea salt and pepper

1 Soak the split peas in cold water to cover overnight, then drain and rinse.
Soak the pearl barley in a separate bowl of cold water for 1 hour, then drain.
2 Cut the lamb fillet roughly into 1cm (½ inch) cubes and place in a large
heavy-based pan with the thyme, barley and split peas. Cover with the stock
and season with a little salt and pepper. Bring to the boil and simmer for
1 hour, skimming from time to time.
3 Meanwhile, cut the leek, carrots, celery, turnip and cabbage roughly into
1cm (½ inch) dice. Add the vegetables, except the cabbage, to the pan and
simmer for another 30 minutes.
4 Add the chopped cabbage and parsley to the soup and simmer for a further
10 minutes. Skim any fat from the surface, check the seasoning and serve.

This comforting, stew-like soup is ideal as a
main course on a cold winter's day, with some
crusty bread. It is also one of those dishes that
almost tastes better the day after it's made.

Brown Windsor soup

Serves 4–6

300g (11oz) braising steak

2–3 tbsp vegetable oil

1 onion, peeled and roughly chopped

1 small carrot, peeled and roughly
   chopped

1 small leek, trimmed, roughly
   chopped and rinsed

good knob of butter

2 tbsp plain flour

1 tsp tomato purée

1 garlic clove, peeled and crushed

few thyme sprigs

1 small bay leaf

3 litres (5 pints) beef stock

2 tbsp cream sherry

sea salt and pepper

1 Cut the braising steak into bite-sized pieces. Heat the oil in a large heavy-based saucepan and fry the meat and vegetables, stirring over a high heat until nicely browned.

2 Add the butter to the pan and stir, then add the flour and cook, stirring, for another couple of minutes. Add the tomato purée, garlic, thyme and bay leaf, then gradually add the beef stock, stirring well to avoid lumps. Bring to a simmer, season with salt and pepper, and simmer for 2 hours or until the meat is tender.

3 Whiz the soup in a blender or using a hand-held stick blender until smooth, then strain through a sieve into a clean pan. The soup should be rich in flavour and a nice brown colour; if not, simmer for a little longer to concentrate the flavour.

4 Adjust the seasoning if necessary, and stir the sherry into the soup just before serving.

This traditional soup is out of favour these days, but it can be a real winter warmer. You could easily cheat and blend braised beef or oxtail with stock and a little cream sherry.

London particular

Serves 4–6

250g (9oz) dried green split peas

25g (1oz) butter

1 onion, peeled and roughly chopped

few thyme sprigs

1–1.5 litres (1¾–2½ pints) ham stock,
plus about 150g (5oz) leftover ham
(see page 175)

pepper (and sea salt if necessary)

1 Soak the dried split peas in cold water to cover overnight or according to the packet instructions.

2 Drain the split peas. Melt the butter in a heavy-based saucepan, add the onion and cook gently for 5 minutes or so until soft, without allowing it to colour. Add the thyme sprigs, split peas and 1 litre (1¾ pints) of the ham stock. Bring to the boil and skim, then add some pepper (but no salt).

3 Simmer for 1 hour or until the peas are cooked, topping up with more stock or water as necessary. The cooking time will depend on the age of the peas. They should be cooked until they are soft and beginning to fall apart.

4 Whiz the soup in a blender or using a hand-held stick blender to the desired texture – make it as coarse or as smooth as you like and add a little water if it is too thick. (If the soup is too thin, you can simmer it for a little longer to reduce and thicken.) Check the seasoning and add a little salt and more pepper if necessary.

5 Shred the cooked ham trimmings and add to the soup. Reheat in the pan and simmer for a few more minutes before serving.

This thick, warming soup is an ideal way to use the stock from boiled ham and some of the leftover meat. Ham stock can be quite salty, so taste it before you start and dilute with water if necessary.

british starters, snacks and savouries

Summer vegetable salad with goat's cheese

Serves 4

65g (2½oz) shelled fresh or frozen
  peas
100g (3½oz) podded fresh young
  broad beans
100g (3½oz) asparagus tips
65g (2½oz) small salad leaves (1 or
  2 varieties)
small mint leaves, from 2 or 3 sprigs
75g (3oz) soft goat's cheese, broken
  into small pieces
small handful of fine chives,
  trimmed

For the dressing

1 tbsp good quality white wine
  vinegar (preferably Chardonnay)
3 tbsp olive oil
2 tbsp vegetable or corn oil
1 tsp caster sugar
few mint leaves
sea salt and pepper

1 Cook the peas, broad beans and asparagus separately in boiling salted
water until just tender; allow 5–7 minutes for peas, 3–4 minutes for broad
beans, 2–3 minutes for asparagus.

2 Meanwhile, make the dressing. Whiz the wine vinegar, oils, sugar and
mint leaves together in a blender or food processor and season with salt and
pepper to taste.

3 Drain the vegetables, refresh briefly in cold water to stop the cooking and
drain again. (If the broad beans aren't as small and young as they might be,
slip them out of their skins after cooking.) Toss the warm drained vegetables
with a spoonful or two of the dressing and season with salt and pepper.

4 Combine the salad leaves and mint leaves in a bowl and lightly dress with
some of the dressing. Divide between serving plates, scatter the vegetables
on top and spoon over a little more dressing. Arrange the pieces of goat's
cheese on top and finish with the chives.

Asparagus with hollandaise sauce

Serves 4–6
1kg (2¼lb) medium to thick
   asparagus

For the hollandaise
3 tbsp white wine vinegar
1 small shallot, peeled and chopped
few tarragon sprigs
1 bay leaf
5 black peppercorns
200g (7oz) unsalted butter
3 small egg yolks
sea salt and white pepper

1 To prepare the asparagus, cut or break off the woody ends. Peel the stalks with a fine swivel vegetable peeler, starting about 5cm (2 inches) down from the tips. Set aside.

2 To make the hollandaise, put the wine vinegar, shallot, tarragon, bay leaf, black peppercorns and 3 tbsp water in a pan and boil to reduce to 2 tsp. Strain and cool. Melt the butter in a small pan and simmer for 5 minutes. Allow to cool a little, then pour off the clarified butter into a bowl, leaving the sediment behind.

3 Put the egg yolks into a small bowl with half of the reduced vinegar and stand the bowl over a pan of gently simmering water. Whisk until the mixture begins to thicken and become frothy. Slowly trickle in the butter, whisking constantly; if added too quickly the sauce will separate. When you've added two thirds of the butter, add some or all of the remaining vinegar reduction to taste. Then add the rest of the butter. The vinegar should just cut the oiliness of the butter. Season with salt and white pepper, cover with cling film and leave in a warm, not hot, place until needed. The hollandaise sauce can be reheated over a bowl of hot water and lightly whisked again to serve.

4 Add the asparagus to a pan of gently simmering, salted water and cook until tender, allowing about 4–5 minutes for finger-thick spears. Drain and serve with the hollandaise sauce.

Boiled duck's egg with asparagus soldiers

Serves 4
900g (2lb) medium to thick
   asparagus
4 duck eggs (or ordinary hen's eggs)
sea salt

1 To prepare the asparagus, cut or break off the woody ends. Peel the stalks with a fine swivel vegetable peeler, starting about 5cm (2 inches) down from the tips. Set aside.
2 Carefully lower the eggs into a pan of boiling water and boil for 6 minutes for duck eggs (or 4–5 minutes for ordinary hen's eggs).
3 Meanwhile, add the asparagus to a pan of boiling salted water and cook for 4–5 minutes until tender.
4 Cut the tops from the eggs and sit the eggs in egg cups. Drain the asparagus and arrange in bundles next to the eggs, for dipping. Serve with a little pile of Maldon sea salt.

Fresh asparagus is an excellent foil for rich, soft-boiled duck eggs. Serve as an elegant starter, brunch or snack.

Deep-fried whitebait

Serves 4
300g (11oz) frozen whitebait
vegetable or corn oil, for deep-frying
4 tbsp plain flour
1 tsp sea salt, plus extra to sprinkle
good pinch of cayenne pepper
125ml (4fl oz) milk
lemon wedges, to serve

1 Preheat the oven to low, 110°C (fan oven 100°C), gas mark ¼, to keep the whitebait warm once you have deep-fried them. Heat an 8–9cm (3½ inch) depth of oil in a deep-fat fryer or heavy-based deep saucepan to 175–180°C.

2 Mix the flour, salt and cayenne pepper together in one bowl. Pour the milk into another. The next stage is a bit of a messy job. While the whitebait are still frozen, toss them first in the flour to coat, shake off any excess and put them into the milk. Drain them from the milk and then drop them back into the flour. Once again, shake off any excess flour and put them on a plate or tray ready to fry.

3 Cook the whitebait in two or three batches, depending on the size of your deep-fryer or pan, for 2–3 minutes each, stirring occasionally with a slotted spoon so they don't stick together. Remove with the slotted spoon and drain on kitchen paper. Keep warm in the low oven while you cook the rest.

4 Divide the deep-fried whitebait between warm plates and sprinkle with a little salt. Serve at once, with lemon wedges.

Whitebait are the small fry of herrings and sprats. I find these fish are best cooked from frozen; shake them in a dry tea towel to lose excess ice glaze before coating and deep-frying.

Soused mackerel

Serves 4

8 mackerel fillets, each about
   75–100g (3–3½oz), trimmed
2 small onions, peeled and cut into
   thin rings
1 carrot, peeled and thinly sliced on
   the diagonal

1 bay leaf
8 peppercorns
½ tsp sea salt
½ tsp fennel seeds
125ml (4fl oz) white wine vinegar

1 Preheat the oven to 180°C (fan oven 160°C), gas mark 4. Check over the mackerel fillets and remove any small pin bones with tweezers. Roll up the fillets, skin-side out, and secure each with a cocktail stick. Put into an ovenproof dish, not too close together.

2 Put all the rest of the ingredients into a saucepan with 90ml (3fl oz) water and bring to the boil.

3 Pour the vinegar mixture over the mackerel fillets, cover the dish with a lid or foil and cook in the oven for 25 minutes. Leave to cool in the dish.

4 Serve the soused mackerel with brown bread and butter.

This is an old way of preserving your catch, and the end result (which will keep for up to a week in the fridge) is delicious with brown bread and butter for supper.

Oysters with shallot vinegar

Illustrated on previous pages

Serves 4

24 oysters

seaweed and/or crushed ice, to serve

For the shallot vinegar

4 shallots, peeled and very finely
    diced

100ml (3½fl oz) good quality red
    wine vinegar

1 First make the shallot vinegar. Mix the shallots and red wine vinegar together in a bowl and set aside to infuse for 1 hour.

2 Now prise open the oysters. Lay an oyster in a folded tea towel on a surface with the flat shell uppermost and the pointed hinge facing towards you. Holding the oyster down with the cloth, force the tip of the oyster knife into the hinge of the shell, carefully moving it from side to side until you can feel the shell loosening – it will take some force.

3 Keep the knife in the shell, twisting it a little and run it along the top of the flat shell until you feel the muscle, which attaches the oyster to the shell. Cut through this to detach the top shell.

4 Remove any bits of shell that may be on the oyster flesh, but don't pour away the natural juices. You can loosen the oyster meat from the curved shell for your guests and flip it over or let them do it themselves. Line four plates with seaweed and/or crushed ice and place a small bowl of shallot vinegar in the centre. Arrange 6 oysters on each plate and serve.

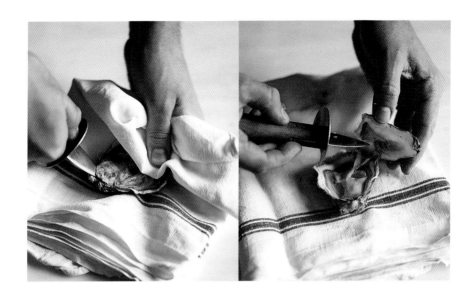

Opening or 'shucking' oysters can be tricky. If you haven't tackled it before, I suggest you buy an oyster knife with a guard to protect your hand. The season officially starts in September and lasts through the following months with an 'r'. However, October is generally held to be the best time to start eating them.

Dressed crab

Illustrated on previous pages

Serves 4

2 cooked crabs, each about 1kg (2¼lb)

For the crab mayonnaise (optional)

juice of ½ lemon, or to taste

2 tsp tomato ketchup

1 tsp Worcestershire sauce

1 tsp English mustard

65–75g (2½–3oz) brown bread, crusts
removed and torn into small pieces

2–3 tbsp good quality mayonnaise

sea salt and white pepper

To serve

lemon wedges

brown bread and butter

1 First you need to get the meat out of the crab. Lay the crab on its back and twist off the claws. Crack the claws open with a mallet or rolling pin and remove the white meat.

2 Now turn the main body on its back and twist off the pointed flap. Push the tip of a table knife between the main shell and the body section and twist the blade to separate the two, then push the body up and remove from the outer shell. Remove the dead man's fingers (the feather like, grey gills attached to the body) and discard.

3 Split the body section in half with a heavy knife and then split each half in two. Now you need to be patient and pick out the white meat from the little cavities in the body using a lobster pick or a teaspoon. Go through the white meat carefully to make sure there are no residual bits of shell.

4 Loosen the brown meat in the main shell with a teaspoon and scoop it out into a bowl. Check that there are no fragments of shell, then put to one side. Scrub the shell if you wish to serve the crab in it.

5 To prepare the crab mayonnaise if required, put the brown meat, lemon juice, ketchup, Worcestershire sauce and mustard into a blender or food processor and whiz until smooth. Add the bread and process again until smooth. Transfer to a bowl, whisk in the mayonnaise and season with salt and pepper. Add a little more lemon juice, if necessary. Refrigerate for an hour or so before serving.

6 To prepare the main shell for serving, look for the natural line on the underside. Push the open edge gently with your fingers into the shell and it will break along the line, leaving a neat shell. Wash the shell under warm water and pat dry. Spoon the brown meat or the brown crab mayonnaise, into the centre and the white meat on either side. Serve with lemon wedges and brown bread and butter.

You can't beat freshly cooked crab with good mayonnaise. I prefer to tackle the crab myself, armed with crackers and a finger bowl rather than buy ready-prepared crab, which can be disappointing. Fresh white meat has a superb taste and texture. The brown meat, however, can be a little dry, but combining it with a few flavourings and some mayonnaise transforms it into something else.

Potted salmon with pickled cucumber

Serves 4–6

325g (11oz) salmon fillet, skinned
75g (3oz) smoked salmon, finely
    chopped
125g (4oz) unsalted butter, softened
1 tbsp thick yogurt
½ tbsp finely chopped chives
juice of ½ lemon
good pinch of cayenne pepper

For the pickling cucumber

1 medium cucumber
200ml (7fl oz) white wine vinegar
2 large shallots, peeled and thinly
    sliced
1 tsp mustard seeds
4 tsp caster sugar
1 tbsp finely chopped dill
a little olive oil, to taste
sea salt and coarsely ground black
    pepper

1 First prepare the pickled cucumber. Halve the cucumber lengthways, scoop out the seeds, then slice thinly at an angle and put into a bowl. Meanwhile, put the vinegar, shallots, mustard seeds, sugar, salt and pepper into a pan and bring to the boil, then remove from the heat and leave to cool a little. Pour over the cucumbers and set aside for 1 hour, stirring every so often. Mix in the dill. Transfer to a sterilised Kilner jar, seal and store in a cool dark place, or keep in a covered bowl in the fridge if using within a few days.
2 Check over the salmon and remove any small pin bones with tweezers. Put the salmon into a saucepan, just cover with cold water and add 1 tsp salt. Bring to the boil, lower the heat and simmer for 2 minutes. Remove from the heat and leave the fish to cool in the liquid; it will finish cooking in the residual heat.
3 Drain the cooled salmon and flake the flesh into a bowl. In another bowl, carefully mix the smoked salmon and softened butter. Add the yogurt, chives and lemon juice, season with salt and cayenne pepper, and mix well. Fold in the flaked salmon, being careful not to break the pieces up too much.
4 Before serving, drain off the liquid from the pickled cucumber (you can save it for another batch). Toss the drained cucumbers with a little olive oil.
5 Serve the potted salmon at room temperature, not refrigerator-cold, either naturally spooned on to a plate or in little ramekins, with hot toast and the pickled cucumbers.

Jellied ham with piccalilli

Illustrated on previous pages

Serves 6–8

1 ham hock, about 1kg (2¼lb), or a
   700g (1½lb) ham joint, soaked
   overnight in plenty of cold water
few thyme sprigs
1 bay leaf
2 onions, peeled and quartered
3 celery stalks
10 black peppercorns
3–4 sheets of leaf gelatine (the
   smaller quantity if using a hock)
2 tbsp chopped parsley

For the piccalilli

1 medium cucumber, halved and
   deseeded
½ large cauliflower, cut into small
   florets
1 onion, peeled and chopped
1 tbsp salt
150g (5oz) caster sugar
65g (2½oz) English mustard
½ tsp ground turmeric
1 small chilli, deseeded and finely
   chopped
150ml (¼ pint) malt vinegar
125ml (4fl oz) white wine vinegar
1 tbsp cornflour

1 First make the piccalilli. Cut the cucumber into 1cm (½ inch) pieces. Halve the cauliflower florets and place in a dish with the cucumber and onion. Sprinkle with the salt and leave for 1 hour. Rinse well, drain and put into a bowl. Put the sugar, mustard, turmeric, chilli and vinegars into a saucepan. Dissolve over a low heat, then simmer for 2–3 minutes. Mix the cornflour with 150ml (¼ pint) water and whisk into the vinegar mixture. Simmer gently, stirring, for 5 minutes. Pour the hot liquid over the vegetables and leave to cool. Pour into sterilised jars and refrigerate for at least a week before use, or up to 6 months.

2 Put the ham into a large saucepan with the thyme, bay leaf, onions, celery and peppercorns. Add water to cover, bring to the boil and simmer until the ham is tender, about 2 hours depending on the cut and size (refer to pack guidelines if applicable). Remove the ham from the liquid and leave to cool.

3 Skim the cooking liquor, measure 350ml (12fl oz) and bring to the boil in a pan. Meanwhile, soak the gelatine in cold water for few minutes to soften, then squeeze out excess water. Remove the liquor from the heat and add the gelatine, with the parsley, stirring to dissolve. Leave until cool, but not set.

4 Meanwhile, remove the ham from the bone and cut roughly into 1cm (½ inch) cubes, discarding any fat and gristle, and put it into a bowl. Mix in a little of the cooled jellied liquor and pack into a 1.2 litre (2 pint) terrine. Top up with the remaining liquor (you may not need all of it). Cover with cling film and leave to set in the fridge overnight.

5 To serve, briefly dip the terrine into a bowl of boiling water and invert on to a chopping board to turn out. With a carving knife, cut it into 2cm (¾ inch) thick slices. Serve on individual plates, with the piccalilli.

This is a great way to use some of the meat from a home-cooked ham joint. Make the piccalilli at least a week ahead, and soak the ham overnight before cooking as it can sometimes be salty.

Chicken livers with wild mushrooms

Illustrated on previous pages

Serves 4

300g (11oz) fresh chicken livers,
  halved if large
2–3 tbsp vegetable oil
300g (11oz) wild mushrooms, cleaned
  and halved or quartered if large

2 garlic cloves, crushed
100g (3½oz) butter
2 tbsp chopped parsley
sea salt and pepper

1 Check over the chicken livers and remove any white sinews. Also look out for, and remove any green bile sac, which can leave a rather nasty taste in the mouth. Pat the chicken livers dry on some kitchen paper and season lightly with salt and pepper.

2 Heat 1 tbsp oil in a heavy-based frying pan until just beginning to smoke and quickly fry the livers for a minute on each side, until nicely coloured but still pink inside, then transfer them to a plate.

3 Clean the pan, add a little oil and heat it again. Add the mushrooms and garlic, season with salt and pepper and fry over a high heat for a few minutes, stirring occasionally until the mushrooms begin to soften and are lightly coloured.

4 Return the chicken livers to the pan with the mushrooms and add the butter. Cook for another minute or two, then add the parsley and stir well. Ideally the chicken livers should still be just a little pink inside. Spoon on to warm plates and serve straightaway.

Wild mushrooms are increasingly available in shops these days. Unless it is really necessary to wash them, just trim and brush or wipe to clean. If unavailable, oyster mushrooms are probably the best alternative.

Angels on horseback

Serves 4

4 rashers of rindless streaky bacon, cut as thinly as possible

8 large oysters, removed from the shell (see page 64)

1 tbsp vegetable oil

65g (2½oz) butter

2 shallots, peeled and finely diced

1 tbsp chopped parsley

4 slices of baguette, cut at an angle, each 1cm (½ inch) thick

1 Cut the bacon rashers across in half and, with the back of a knife on a chopping board, stretch the bacon as thinly as it will go, until almost translucent. Pat the oysters dry with some kitchen paper and wrap each one securely in a piece of bacon.

2 Heat a little oil in a heavy-based frying pan and quickly fry the wrapped oysters over a high heat for a minute or so on each side. Remove the bacon-wrapped oysters from the pan and set aside.

3 Melt the butter in the pan and add the shallots. Fry over a low heat for a minute or so, without allowing them to colour, then add the parsley and remove from the heat.

4 Meanwhile, toast the bread on both sides, arrange 2 wrapped oysters on each slice and spoon the shallots and parsley over to serve.

You may have heard of 'devils on horseback', where prunes are the 'devil' wrapped in bacon. Here, oysters replace prunes as the 'angel' and they are served on toast. A classic savoury, these are also ideal canapés and party snacks.

Soft roes on toast

Serves 4
450–500g (about 1lb) herring soft
  roes
150g (5oz) butter
flour, to dust
4 slices of bread (cut from a small
  bloomer)
65g (2½oz) drained capers
1 tbsp chopped parsley
sea salt and pepper

1 Pat the roes dry on kitchen paper. Heat a knob of butter in a large (or two smaller) non-stick frying pan(s). Season the roes and flour lightly, shaking off excess. Add to the pan and cook over a medium heat on both sides until the roes turn golden brown and curl up.
2 Meanwhile, toast the bread on both sides. Pile the cooked roes on the toast. Melt the rest of the butter in the pan, add the capers and parsley, then spoon over the roes and serve.

Herring roes, soft roes or milts, are normally sold frozen or thawed, but are sometimes available fresh during the spring and early summer. Treat frozen ones correctly and no one will know the difference.

Scotch woodcock

Serves 4

25g (1oz) butter, plus extra to spread

4 eggs, beaten

1 tbsp double cream

4 slices of bread (cut from a small bloomer)

sea salt and pepper

To serve

10 anchovy fillets in oil, drained and cut in half lengthways

10–12 large capers, drained and washed

1 Melt the butter in a heavy-based pan, add the eggs and cream with seasoning, and stir with a wooden spoon over a medium heat. The eggs should be nice and creamy when they are cooked.

2 Meanwhile, toast the bread on both sides and butter it. Spoon the eggs on to the toast and arrange the anchovies in a lattice on top. Scatter the capers over to serve.

This is another savoury rarely seen on menus these days. It's good as a light snack or even for brunch. A few of the anchovies can be mashed and folded into the cooked eggs for a more savoury flavour.

Welsh rabbit

Serves 4

4 tbsp Guinness

5 tbsp double cream

150g (5oz) Cheddar cheese, grated

1 egg yolk

2 tsp Worcestershire sauce, or more
to taste

1 tsp English mustard

8 thick slices of bread (cut from a
small bloomer)

sea salt and pepper

1 Well in advance of serving, pour the Guinness into a small pan and simmer until reduced by half. Add the cream and simmer again until reduced by two thirds. Leave to cool.
2 Preheat the grill to medium. Add the cheese, egg yolk, Worcestershire sauce and mustard to the reduced Guinness and season with salt and pepper to taste.
3 Toast the bread on both sides, then spread the cheese mixture on top, about 1cm (½ inch) thick, and to the edges to prevent these burning. Grill until the topping is nicely browned, then serve.

For years I thought it was 'rarebit', but I was persuaded otherwise by various reputable food writers. Anyway, refined cheese on toast with a few savoury additions is what it is.

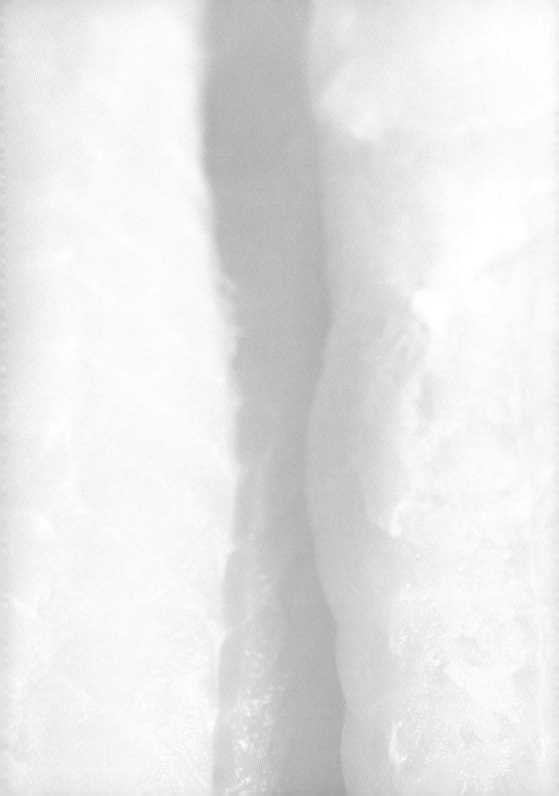

british
fish and
seafood

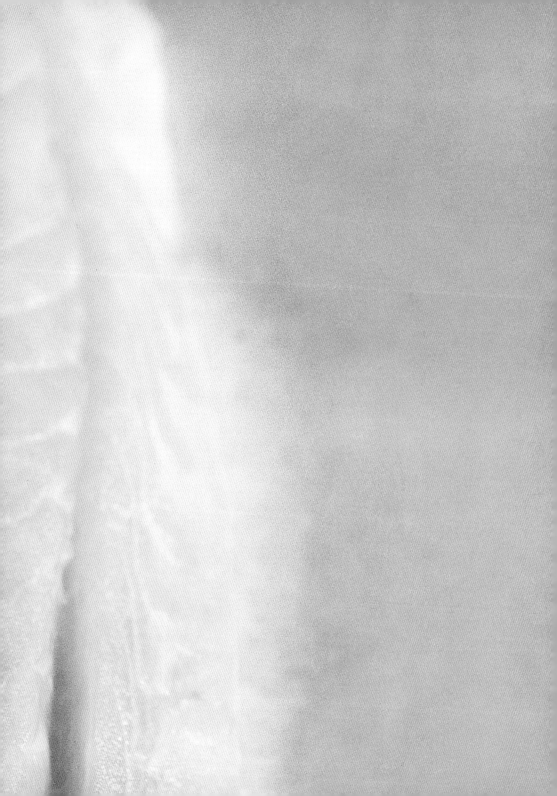

Jerusalem artichoke, lobster and bacon salad

Serves 4

500g (1lb 2oz) Jerusalem artichokes,
  peeled
2 cooked lobsters, each about 500g
  (1lb 2oz)
3 tbsp good quality mayonnaise
1 tbsp chopped chervil
8 thin rashers of rindless streaky
  bacon
sea salt and white pepper

For the dressing

1 tsp tomato ketchup
2 tsp white wine vinegar
1 tsp Dijon mustard
3 tbsp olive oil

1 Cook the artichokes in boiling salted water for 10–15 minutes or until tender to the point of a knife. Drain them in a colander and return to the pan over a low heat for a minute or so, to drive off any excess water. Put them into a bowl and leave to cool.

2 Meanwhile, remove the head from the lobster and the main body shell by squeezing the shell in the palm of your hand until you feel it break, then carefully remove the meat intact by prising the shell open with your thumbs. Crack the claws with a mallet or rolling pin and extract the meat. Cut the lobster tail meat in half lengthways.

3 Preheat the grill. Mash the artichokes coarsely with a fork, then mix in the mayonnaise and three quarters of the chervil. Season with salt and pepper to taste.

4 Make the dressing by whisking all the ingredients together, seasoning with a little salt and pepper.

5 Spoon the Jerusalem artichoke evenly into a pile in the centre of four plates. Place a half lobster tail on top of each serving, with the claw meat. Grill the bacon until crisp and arrange on the lobster. Spoon the dressing around and sprinkle with the remaining chervil to serve.

Herb baked queen scallops

Serves 4

32 queen scallops (in the half shell)

For the herb crust

50g (2oz) butter

2 garlic cloves, peeled and crushed

1 tbsp chopped parsley

40g (1½oz) fresh white breadcrumbs

sea salt and pepper

For the garlic butter

100g (3½oz) butter

2 garlic cloves, peeled and crushed

1 To make the herb crust, melt the butter in a pan and gently cook the garlic for a minute without allowing it to colour. Stir in the chopped parsley and breadcrumbs, and season with salt and pepper. Set aside.

2 Preheat the grill to high. Lay the scallops on their half shell on a grill tray and scatter with the herb crust. Cook under the hot grill for 3–4 minutes until lightly coloured.

3 Meanwhile, make the garlic butter. Melt the butter in a pan until foaming, then add the crushed garlic. Remove from the heat and spoon over the scallops to serve.

Queen scallops are quite small, about the size of a golf ball, and they are a bit tedious to prepare, but you can buy them in the half shell, ready cleaned. If you can't find queen scallops, 24 medium ordinary scallops will do.

Fish and chips

Illustrated on previous pages

4 quality fish fillets, such as cod,
    haddock, hake or plaice, each
    150–175g (5–6oz)
800g–1kg (1¾ –2¼lb) potatoes,
    peeled
vegetable oil, to deep-fry
flour, to dust
sea salt
For the batter
7g (¼oz) fast-action dried yeast
300ml (½ pint) milk

75g (3oz) plain flour
75g (3oz) cornflour
pinch of cayenne pepper
¼ tsp baking powder
1 small egg yolk
For the minted pea purée
25g (1oz) butter, plus a knob to serve
1 large shallot, peeled and diced
400g (14oz) frozen peas
100ml (3½fl oz) vegetable stock
6–8 mint leaves

1 To make the batter for the fish, dissolve the yeast in 3 tbsp of the milk and
leave in a warm place for 10 minutes. Combine the remaining ingredients in
a bowl and beat until smooth, then add the yeast and some salt. Cover and
leave to ferment for 1½–2 hours. If the batter is too thick, add a little water.
2 To make the pea purée, heat the butter in a pan and gently cook the shallot
until soft. Add the peas, stock and mint, season and simmer for 12 minutes.
Whiz in a food processor until smooth, check the seasoning and set aside.
3 For the chips, cut the potatoes into 1cm (½ inch) slices, then into 1cm
(½ inch) thick chips. Rinse in water and drain thoroughly on kitchen paper.
Heat the oil to 120°C in a deep-fat fryer or heavy-based saucepan (no more
than half full). Blanch your chips in the hot oil, 2 or 3 handfuls at a time,
until soft but not coloured, then remove, drain and set aside.
4 To cook the fish, heat a 10cm (4 inch) depth of oil in a deep-fat fryer or
heavy saucepan to 175–180°C. Remove any small bones from the fish fillets,
then flour lightly. Dip in the batter, then fry in the oil, two at a time for
4–5 minutes until browned. Drain and keep warm on a tray in a warm oven
while you cook the rest.
5 To finish the chips, heat the oil to 175–180°C and re-fry them in the same
way until crisp and golden. Drain and season lightly with salt. If necessary,
keep warm and crisp – scattered on a baking tray in a warm oven.
6 The fish and chips are best eaten as soon as possible after frying. Serve
with the minted pea purée, which can be warmed through with a knob of
butter if necessary.

Skate with shrimps and capers

Serves 4

4 skate wings, each about 200–250g (7–9oz), skinned and trimmed
flour, to dust
1–2 tbsp vegetable or corn oil
150g (5oz) unsalted butter
juice of 1 lemon

65g (2½oz) drained good quality capers, rinsed
75–100g (3–3½oz) cooked, peeled brown shrimps or prawns
1 tbsp chopped parsley
sea salt and white pepper

1 Season the skate wings and lightly flour them, shaking off excess. Heat the oil in a large heavy-based frying pan (preferably non-stick) and add the skate in a single layer. Cook for 3–5 minutes on each side until golden, adding about one third of the butter to the pan when they are almost cooked (to give them a nice brown colour). When the skate wings are done, remove from the pan and keep warm.

2 Wipe the pan out with some kitchen paper, add the rest of the butter and heat it gently until it begins to foam. Add the lemon juice, capers, shrimps or prawns and parsley, and remove from the heat.

3 Put the skate on warm plates and spoon the shrimp and caper butter evenly over the top. Serve with spinach and good buttery mash.

Note If you are cooking several pieces of skate, you may find it easier to brown them quickly on each side and finish cooking in the oven preheated to 200°C (fan oven 180°C), gas mark 6 for about 10 minutes.

Some people are put off skate because it is served 'on the bone', or rather on its cartilage framework. In fact, skate is easy to eat because the flesh easily forks away from the 'bones'.

Poached salmon and asparagus salad

Serves 4

600g (1¼lb) salmon fillet, skinned
150–200g (5–7oz) thin asparagus tips
75–100g (3–3½oz) small salad leaves,
  such as corn salad, oak leaf, baby
  spinach
10–12 chives, cut into short lengths

For the poaching liquid

3 tbsp olive oil
few thyme sprigs
1 bay leaf
1 tsp fennel seeds
½ glass of white wine
200ml (7fl oz) fish stock

For the dressing

1 tbsp good quality white wine
  vinegar (preferably Chardonnay)
1 tsp thin honey
1 tsp grainy mustard
4 tbsp olive oil
1 tsp chopped chervil
1 tsp chopped chives
sea salt and white pepper

1 First prepare the poaching liquid. Put the olive oil, thyme, bay leaf, fennel seeds, white wine and fish stock into a wide, shallow saucepan. Season with salt and pepper, bring to the boil and simmer for 2–3 minutes.

2 Meanwhile, remove any small pin bones from the salmon with tweezers. Put the fish into the liquid and lay a piece of greaseproof paper directly on top of it. Simmer very gently for 3–4 minutes, then remove from the heat. Leave the salmon to cool in the liquid until required.

3 Bring a pan of salted water to the boil, add the asparagus tips and cook for 2–3 minutes until tender. Remove with a slotted spoon and leave on a plate to cool a little.

4 To make the dressing, whisk the wine vinegar with the honey and mustard. Gradually whisk in the olive oil and herbs, and season with salt and pepper.

5 Remove the salmon from the cooking liquid and pat dry with kitchen paper. Arrange the salad leaves on plates, then flake the salmon into pieces over the leaves. Arrange the asparagus on top, season lightly and spoon over the dressing. Scatter the chives on top.

Grilled mackerel with gooseberry sauce

Serves 4

4 whole mackerel, each about 200g
  (7oz), cleaned and heads removed
good knob of butter
250g (9oz) gooseberries, topped and
  tailed
2 tsp caster sugar
½ glass of white wine
150ml (¼ pint) double cream
vegetable oil, to brush
sea salt and white pepper

1 Make 4 or 5 slashes diagonally across each mackerel with a sharp knife, scoring through the skin into the flesh. Season with salt and pepper. Preheat the grill to high.

2 Melt the butter in a heavy-based pan. Add the gooseberries with the sugar, then cover and cook over a medium heat for about 5–6 minutes, stirring every so often, until the gooseberries are soft and have broken down. Add the white wine, turn up the heat and cook until all the liquid has evaporated. Add the cream, bring to the boil and simmer until the sauce has reduced by half and thickened. Depending on the gooseberries, you may need to add a little more sugar.

3 Meanwhile, brush the mackerel with a little oil and cook under the hot grill for about 6–8 minutes. Transfer to warm plates and serve the gooseberry sauce separately, or on the plate if you like.

Mackerel are available through the summer months and must be eaten as fresh as possible. Gooseberry sauce sounds like an odd thing to combine with fish, but the acidity of the fruit complements mackerel perfectly. Frozen gooseberries can be used.

Fish pie

Illustrated on previous pages

Serves 4–6

250g (9oz) cod or haddock fillet,
   skinned
250g (9oz) salmon fillet, skinned
250g (9oz) smoked cod or haddock
   fillet
500ml (16fl oz) fish stock
100ml (3½fl oz) white wine
2 tbsp chopped parsley

For the sauce

50g (2oz) butter
50g (2oz) plain flour
175ml (6fl oz) double cream
2 tsp English mustard
½ tbsp Worcestershire sauce
1 tsp anchovy essence
sea salt and white pepper

For the topping

1.5kg (3¼lb) potatoes, peeled, cooked
   and mashed (see page 212)
50g (2oz) butter, softened
about 1–2 tbsp milk
25g (1oz) fresh white breadcrumbs
25g (1oz) grated Cheddar cheese

1 Remove any small pin bones from the fish fillets, then cut roughly into
3cm (1¼ inch) chunks. Pour the fish stock and wine into a large pan and
bring to a simmer. Add the fish and poach gently in the liquid for 2 minutes.
Drain in a colander over a bowl to save the liquor and leave to cool.
2 To make the sauce, melt the butter in a heavy-based pan over a low heat,
then stir in the flour. Gradually stir in the reserved poaching liquor. Bring
to the boil and simmer gently for 15 minutes.

3 Add the cream and continue to simmer for 10 minutes or so until the sauce has a thick coating consistency. Stir in the mustard, Worcestershire sauce, anchovy essence, and seasoning if required. Set aside to cool for about 15 minutes.

4 Gently fold the cooked fish and parsley into the sauce, and spoon into a large pie dish to about 3cm (1¼ inches) from the rim. Leave to stand for about 30 minutes.

5 Preheat the oven to 180°C (fan oven 160°C), gas mark 4. To prepare the topping, mix the butter and milk into the mashed potato and season with a little salt and pepper. Spoon the potato over the pie and bake for 30 minutes, then scatter the breadcrumbs and cheese on top and bake for a further 15 minutes until golden.

A medley of fish in a piquant sauce is baked under a cheesy potato crust for a comforting pie that's best served simply with spinach or peas. Make individual pies if you prefer.

Fish cakes with tartare sauce

Illustrated on previous pages

Serves 4

325g (11oz) skinless fish fillets, such as salmon, smoked haddock and/or white fish, such as cod or hake
325g (11oz) simple mashed potato, without added milk or butter (page 212)
½ tbsp anchovy essence
½ tbsp English mustard
1 tbsp chopped parsley
1 tbsp chopped chives
flour, to dust
1 medium egg, beaten
50–65g (2–2½oz) fresh white breadcrumbs
vegetable oil, to fry
sea salt and white pepper

For the tartare sauce

25g (1oz) gherkins, finely chopped
25g (1oz) capers, rinsed and finely chopped
½ tbsp chopped parsley
4 tbsp mayonnaise
squeeze of lemon juice

1 Poach the fish gently in salted water for 3–4 minutes, then drain and allow to cool. Flake the fish, checking for any small pin bones as you do so. In a bowl, mix half of the fish with the potato, anchovy essence, mustard, parsley, chives and salt and pepper until smooth. Gently fold in the remaining fish.
2 Shape the mixture into 4 large round cakes or 8 small ones and refrigerate for about 1 hour. Meanwhile, mix together the ingredients for the tartare sauce in a bowl, cover and set aside.
3 Take 3 shallow bowls, put the flour in one, the egg in another and the breadcrumbs in the third. Lightly flour the fish cakes, dip them into the beaten egg, then into the breadcrumbs, shaking off excess each time. Shallow-fry the fish cakes in a 1cm (½ inch) depth of hot oil until crisp and golden, turning halfway through cooking, or deep-fry in oil at 175–180ºC. Drain on kitchen paper and serve with the tartare sauce.

Fish cakes are an excellent way to use cheaper varieties of fish and off-cuts. You can make mini-versions of these to serve with drinks if you like.

Baked herrings with mustard and oats

Serves 4

40g (1½oz) butter

2 shallots, peeled and finely chopped

finely grated zest of ½ unwaxed lemon

40g (1½oz) fresh white breadcrumbs

40g (1½oz) oat flakes

1 tbsp chopped parsley

4 herring fillets, each about 150g (5oz), or 8 smaller ones

1 tbsp grainy mustard

sea salt and pepper

1 Preheat the oven to 200°C (fan oven 180°C), gas mark 6. Melt the butter in a pan and gently cook the shallots for a couple of minutes until soft. Transfer to a food processor with the lemon zest, breadcrumbs, oats and parsley. Season with salt and pepper and process for about 20 seconds.

2 Check over the herring fillets and remove any small bones, then place on a baking tray, skin-side up. Spread the mustard evenly over the fillets and spoon the oat mixture on top, pressing it down with the back of the spoon. Bake for 15–20 minutes until cooked. Serve with hot buttered new potatoes.

Herrings were plentiful and cheap around our coastlines in times past, especially along the East Anglian coast. But now that herring fishing is restricted in the North Sea because of overfishing, these fish are less common.

Kedgeree

Serves 4

350g (12oz) undyed smoked haddock
   fillet
150g (5oz) basmati rice
1 tbsp chopped parsley
3 medium eggs, hard-boiled, shelled
   and chopped

For the curry sauce

25g (1oz) butter
2 shallots, peeled and finely chopped
small piece of fresh root ginger,
   peeled and finely chopped
1 garlic clove, peeled and crushed
¼ tsp ground turmeric
¼ tsp ground cumin
½ tsp curry powder
½ tsp fennel seeds
few curry leaves
pinch of saffron threads
100ml (3½fl oz) fish stock
400ml (14fl oz) double cream
sea salt and pepper

1 First make the curry sauce. Melt the butter in a heavy-based pan, add the shallots, ginger and garlic and cook gently until softened, without allowing them to colour. Add the ground spices, fennel seeds, curry leaves and saffron threads, and cook for another minute to release their flavours. Add the fish stock, bring to the boil and allow it to reduce by half. Pour in the cream and simmer until reduced by half. Blend the sauce in a blender or using a hand-held stick blender until smooth, then pass it through a fine-meshed sieve. Adjust the seasoning, if necessary.

2 Poach the smoked haddock in a pan of gently simmering, lightly salted water for 3–4 minutes, then remove from the heat. Leave the fish to cool in the liquid.

3 Rinse the rice a couple times in cold water to remove excess starch, then cook in plenty of boiling salted water for 12–15 minutes until just tender. Briefly drain the rice in a colander, return it to the pan, put the lid on and leave off the heat for few minutes. This allows the rice to steam dry and gives it a light fluffy texture.

4 To serve the kedgeree, reheat the curry sauce. Drain the smoked haddock and flake the flesh, then add to the sauce with the chopped parsley. Put the rice into a bowl, spoon over the fish and sauce, then scatter over the chopped hard-boiled egg.

british poultry and game

Guide to roasting

Nowadays we seem to be rearing better free-range and corn-fed poultry, which cost more than their battery-reared cousins, but taste far superior. Of course, final flavour is down to the cooking, and a well seasoned bird is a good starting point. A good homemade stuffing will also enhance the flavour – of roast chicken and turkey in particular (see page 128).

Game birds are an autumnal treat. Be it partridge, grouse or pheasant, only young game birds should be selected for roasting and these are best cooked simply, and served pink. Quick roasting at a high temperature will keep smaller birds moist and tender, overcooking will make them dry. If you prefer game well cooked, protect the breasts with streaky bacon rashers, especially pheasant.

For me, spit-roasting is the best way of roasting, as you get a good even heat and the cooking time is shorter. If your oven doesn't have a spit-roaster, you can suspend the bird on a rack that fits in the roasting tin to allow it to cook evenly and crisp up.

Chicken
For a 1.2–1.5kg (2¾–3¼lb) bird, allow 40 minutes per kilo (20 minutes per pound), plus an extra 15 minutes, about 1¼ hours in total, at 200°C (fan oven 180°C), gas mark 6. Allow to rest for 15 minutes before serving.

Turkey
For a 4.5–5.5kg (10–12lb) bird, allow 30 minutes per kilo (15 minutes per pound) at 190°C (fan oven 170°C), gas mark 5. Allow to rest for 30 minutes before serving.

Pheasant
Rub the breasts with butter and cover with streaky bacon or pork fat. Cook for 25 minutes at 200°C (fan oven 180°C), gas mark 6. Allow to rest for 5 minutes before serving.

Grouse, snipe, partridge, wood pigeon

Rub the breasts with butter and roast at a high heat, 220°C (fan oven 200°C), gas mark 7, for 15–20 minutes for pink game, or a little longer for well cooked game. Allow to rest for 5 minutes before serving.

Mallard

Rub the breasts with butter and roast at 220°C (fan oven 200°C), gas mark 7, for 30 minutes for pink game, or a little longer for well cooked game. Allow to rest for 5 minutes before serving.

Pan gravy

Tip out as much of the fat from the roasting tin as you can, then place the tin over a medium heat. Add a splash of dry red or white wine, perhaps dust with a little flour, then stir in a cupful of chicken stock. Scrape up the sediment from the bottom and allow to bubble rapidly for a minute or so. Adjust the seasoning and stir in a knob of butter to give the gravy a sheen.

Note: For a thicker gravy, before you add the butter, stir in a spoonful of cornflour mixed with a little cold water and simmer, stirring, for 1 minute.

Traditional accompaniments, such as crunchy parsnip chips and bread sauce (page 130), and seasonal vegetables are the ideal partners for roast poultry and game.

Parsley and thyme stuffing

Serves 4
50g (2oz) butter
1 onion, peeled and finely chopped
2 tsp chopped thyme
125g (4oz) fresh white breadcrumbs
2 tbsp chopped parsley
sea salt and pepper

1 Heat the butter in a small pan, add the onion and thyme and cook gently for a few minutes until the onion is soft, without allowing it to colour.
2 Remove from the heat and add the breadcrumbs and chopped parsley. Mix well and season generously with salt and pepper.
3 Stuff the neck end of the bird only.

To vary this stuffing, try adding some sautéed chopped chicken livers, or perhaps a little grated lemon zest. Alternatively, replace the thyme with chopped sage or, for a turkey stuffing, add some cooked, chopped chestnuts.

Bread sauce

Serves 4

1 onion, peeled and halved
3 cloves
3 bay leaves
50g (2oz) butter
500ml (16fl oz) milk
pinch of freshly grated nutmeg
100g (3½oz) fresh white
    breadcrumbs
sea salt and pepper

1 Stud one of the onion halves with the cloves, pushing each one through a bay leaf into the onion. Finely dice the other onion half.
2 Heat half of the butter in a saucepan, add the diced onion and cook until soft. Add the milk, studded onion half, nutmeg and seasoning. Bring to the boil, lower the heat and simmer for 15 minutes. Remove from the heat and leave to infuse for 30 minutes, then discard the studded onion.
3 Add the breadcrumbs and simmer for 10 minutes. Whiz a third of the mixture in a blender until smooth, then return to the pan. Heat gently and stir in the remaining butter. Season with salt and pepper to taste.

Parsnip chips

Serves 4

2 parsnips, trimmed
vegetable oil, for deep-frying
sea salt

1 Using a mandolin or swivel vegetable peeler, slice the parsnips as thinly as possible lengthways, rinse well and pat dry with a clean tea towel.
2 Half-fill a deep-fat fryer or deep, heavy-based saucepan with oil and heat to 180°C. Deep-fry the parsnip slices, a handful at a time, for 2–3 minutes until golden, stirring to ensure they don't stick together.
3 Remove and place on kitchen paper to drain and crisp up. Sprinkle with salt and leave in a warm (not hot) place while you cook the rest. Serve the parsnip chips as soon as possible.

Basic gravy

Makes 2 litres (3½ pints)

2kg (4½lb) beef, veal, lamb or
    chicken bones, or a mixture,
    chopped into small pieces
3 onions, peeled and roughly
    chopped
5 carrots, peeled and roughly
    chopped
few celery stalks, chopped
3 leeks, well rinsed and roughly
    chopped
½ head of garlic
1 tbsp tomato purée
2 tbsp plain flour
3–4 litres (5–7 pints) dark meat stock
    (page 21) or ready-made stock
10 black peppercorns
few thyme sprigs
1 bay leaf
1–2 tsp cornflour, mixed with a little
    water (optional)
sea salt and pepper

1 Preheat the oven to 200°C (fan oven 180°C), gas mark 6. Put the chopped bones in a roasting tin with the vegetables and garlic and roast for about 15–20 minutes until golden brown, stirring every so often. Stir in the tomato purée, then sprinkle in the flour and stir well. Roast for another 10 minutes.

2 Put the roasting tin on the hob, add a little of the stock and stir over a low heat, scraping up the sediment from the bottom. Transfer everything to a large saucepan and pour in the rest of the stock to cover. Add the black peppercorns, thyme sprigs and bay leaf. Bring to the boil and skim, then simmer for 2 hours, topping up with water to keep the ingredients covered and skimming occasionally as required.

3 Strain through a fine-meshed sieve into a bowl and remove any fat from the surface. Taste to check the strength and boil to reduce and concentrate the flavour if necessary. If the gravy is not thick enough, stir in the blended cornflour and simmer, stirring, for a few minutes. Check the seasoning before serving.

Make a sizeable quantity of gravy and freeze it in small tubs, ready to defrost quickly for a proper gravy to go with a roast. Keep some frozen in ice-cube trays to use in smaller quantities for enhancing sauces.

Roast Gressingham duck with apple sauce

Serves 4

2 ducks, preferably Gressingham,
   each about 1.5–2kg (3¼–4½lb)
4 garlic cloves
few thyme sprigs
few rosemary sprigs
sea salt and pepper

To serve

Bramley apple sauce (see page 178)
basic gravy (see opposite)

1 Preheat the oven to 220°C (fan oven 200°C), gas mark 7. Place the ducks on a board. Divide the garlic, thyme and rosemary between their cavities and season them inside and out with salt and pepper. Place side by side in a roasting tin and roast for 1 hour.

2 Meanwhile, make the apple sauce. If you get giblets with the duck, then simmer them in the gravy for about 10 minutes.

3 To serve, remove the legs from the duck, then take the breasts off the bone and cut into 3 or 4 slices, or simply cut the birds in half and serve them on the bone. Serve with the apple sauce and gravy.

Apple sauce is a perfect perfect partner for roast duck as it cuts the fat with its sweet and slightly acidic flavour. Roast potatoes in the pan with the duck to absorb the flavours.

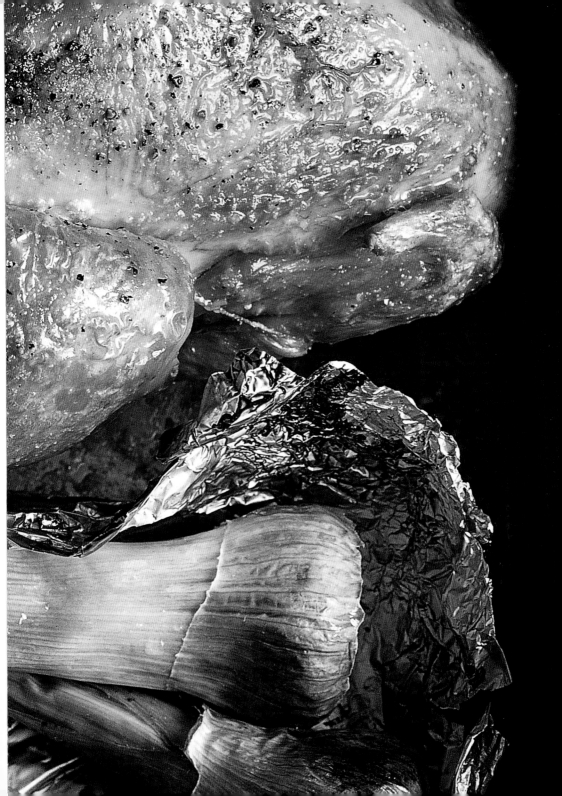

Guinea fowl with Savoy cabbage

Serves 4

6 garlic cloves, peeled
few thyme sprigs
2 guinea fowl, each about 1.1kg
(2½lb)
125g (4oz) butter
4 tbsp red wine
4 tbsp port

150ml (¼ pint) chicken stock
1–2 tsp cornflour (optional)
1kg (2¼lb) Savoy cabbage, trimmed,
cored and roughly chopped
200g (7oz) wild mushrooms, cleaned,
trimmed and halved or quartered
1 tbsp chopped parsley
sea salt and pepper

1 Preheat the oven to 220°C (fan oven 200°C), gas mark 7. Divide the garlic cloves and thyme between the cavities of the two birds. Rub the breasts with 25g (1oz) of the butter and season well with salt and pepper. Place in a roasting tin and roast for 1 hour, basting occasionally.

2 Transfer the guinea fowl to a plate, cover with foil and set aside to rest. Put the roasting tin on a medium heat on the hob, add the red wine and port, and stir well to scrape up any residue on the bottom of the tin. Add the stock and simmer for 3–4 minutes, then strain through a fine sieve. (If you want a thicker gravy, mix the cornflour with a little cold water, add to the gravy and simmer, stirring, for another minute or so, before straining.)

3 While the birds are resting, cook the cabbage in boiling salted water for about 5 minutes until tender. Drain and add 50g (2oz) of the butter, season with salt and pepper and cover with a lid.

4 In the meantime, heat the rest of the butter in a frying pan, add the mushrooms and parsley, season with salt and pepper and sauté over a medium heat until tender. Timing will depend on the type of wild mushrooms; chanterelles take only 30–40 seconds for example, whereas more robust varieties will take a couple of minutes.

5 To serve, remove the legs from the guinea fowl and cut the breasts away from the bone with a sharp knife. Arrange the cabbage on the plates, put the leg and breast meat on top, then pour the sauce around. Spoon the wild mushrooms on top and serve.

Roast pheasant breasts with chestnut stuffing

Serves 4

4 plump boneless pheasant breasts,
   with skin
100g (3½oz) freshly shelled or
   vacuum-packed chestnuts, roughly
   chopped
2 shallots, peeled and finely chopped
40g (1½oz) fresh white breadcrumbs
1 tbsp chopped parsley
25g (1oz) butter, melted
1 tbsp vegetable oil
sea salt and pepper

To serve

creamed Brussels sprouts (page 200)
150ml (¼ pint) pan gravy (page 127,
   made with red wine)
parsnip chips (page 130)

1 Preheat the oven to 200°C (fan oven 180°C), gas mark 6. Lay the pheasant breasts on a board, skin-side down. Remove the fillet and put to one side. With the tip of a sharp knife, cut two incisions away from the centre of the breast to form a pocket. (Here you are just transferring some of the breast meat away from the middle of the breast to make room for the stuffing.)
2 Mix the chestnuts, shallots, breadcrumbs, parsley and melted butter together and season with salt and pepper. Divide the stuffing between the 4 breasts. Flatten the fillet a little with the side of your hand and lay it over the stuffing. Fold the breast meat that you cut previously back into the centre to completely seal in the stuffing.
3 Heat the oil in a roasting tin in the oven for a few minutes. Season the pheasant breasts with salt and pepper, then place in the hot tin and cook in the oven for 5–7 minutes on each side, or until cooked to your liking.
4 Remove the pheasant from the oven, rest for 5 minutes and then carve into slices. Serve on a bed of creamed Brussels sprouts, with the red wine pan gravy and a few parsnip chips.

Roast venison with haggis and neeps

Serves 4

4 trimmed venison saddle fillets,
  each about 150g (5oz)
½ glass of good red wine
6 juniper berries, crushed
few thyme sprigs, chopped
1–2 tbsp vegetable oil
150ml (¼ pint) pan gravy (page 127)
  or basic gravy (page 132)

For the bashed neeps

250g (9oz) parsnips, peeled and
  roughly chopped
250g (9oz) swede, peeled and
  roughly chopped
150–200g (5–7oz) good quality
  haggis, skin removed
good knob of butter
sea salt and pepper

1 A day in advance, put the venison in a stainless steel (or other non-reactive)
bowl with the wine, juniper and thyme, cover with cling film and leave to
marinate overnight.

2 Next day, prepare the neeps: put the parsnips and swede into a pan, add
water to cover and season with salt and pepper. Bring to the boil and simmer
gently for 15–20 minutes until soft enough to mash. Meanwhile, cut the
haggis roughly into 1cm (½ inch) pieces and set aside. Drain the vegetables
in a colander, then tip into a bowl and coarsely mash with a potato masher.
Add the butter and haggis, adjust the seasoning if necessary, and stir well.

3 Remove the venison from the marinade, reserving the liquid. Pat the fillets
dry on some kitchen paper and season with salt and pepper. Heat a little oil
in a heavy-based frying pan and cook the fillets for 2–3 minutes on each side
for medium rare; allow an extra 1–2 minutes each side for medium or longer
if the fillets are very thick. Leave to rest on a warm plate.

4 Meanwhile, boil the marinade in a saucepan rapidly until reduced to about 1 tbsp. Add the gravy and any juices from the venison, and simmer for a minute or so until the sauce is thick, then strain through a fine sieve.
5 Reheat the bashed neeps and spoon into the centre of each warm serving plate. Slice the venison into 4 or 5 pieces and arrange on the neeps, then pour the sauce around.

The saddle is the most tender, readily available cut of venison – and the most expensive. It doesn't take much cooking once removed from the bone, and it eats like the best fillet steak with a little hint of game. I like to marinate it overnight in red wine with crushed juniper berries and thyme leaves.

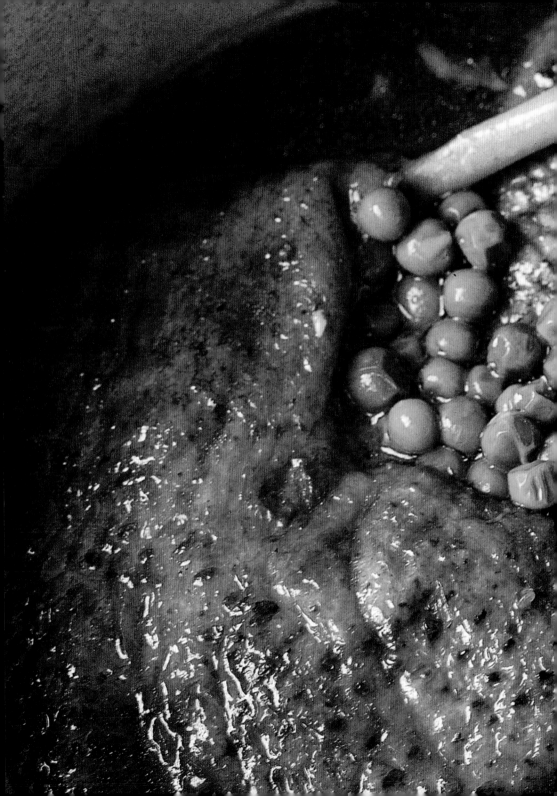

Braised duck with peas

Illustrated on previous pages

Serves 4

2 good quality ducks, such as
   Gressingham, each about 1.5–2kg
   (3¼–4½lb)
200ml (7fl oz) sweet cider
600ml (1 pint) basic gravy (page 132)
600ml (1 pint) chicken stock
few thyme sprigs
1 bay leaf
2 tbsp double cream
200g (7oz) shelled fresh or frozen
   peas, freshly cooked
sea salt and pepper

1 Preheat the oven to 220ºC (fan oven 200°C), gas mark 7. With a heavy
knife, cut the ducks in half lengthways. Cut the parson's nose off and trim
away any excess fat and the backbone where there isn't any meat. Chop the
knuckle from the legs and trim the wing bones, if necessary.

2 Season the birds with salt and pepper, then roast them, skin-side down, in
a roasting tin for 30 minutes. Transfer the ducks to a colander over a bowl
to drain off the fat.

3 Turn the oven down to 170ºC (fan oven 150°C), gas mark 3. Carefully cut
the duck halves in half, where the breast joins the leg.

4 Put the duck pieces into a casserole dish with the cider, gravy, chicken
stock, thyme and bay leaf. Cover with a lid and braise for 1¼ hours. Remove
the ducks from the liquid with a slotted spoon, put them on a warm plate
and cover with foil. Set aside.

5 Transfer the cooking liquid to a saucepan, skim off any fat and simmer
until reduced and thickened. Return the duck to the liquid, add the cream
and peas just to warm through, then check the seasoning and serve.

Buy good quality ducks, like Gressingham or
Barbary, as they are reared with less fat and a
higher meat content. When fresh peas are in
season, make sure you use them – you'll need
to buy about 600g (1¼lb) peas in the pod.

Wild rabbit in cider

Serves 4

12 rabbit legs (back legs only)
40g (1½oz) plain flour, plus extra
    to dust
2 tbsp vegetable oil
25g (1oz) butter

1 onion, peeled and roughly chopped
400ml (14fl oz) dry cider
750ml (1¼ pints) chicken stock
3 tbsp double cream
1 tbsp chopped parsley
sea salt and pepper

1 Halve the rabbit legs at the joint, then lightly flour them and season with salt and pepper. Heat the oil in a frying pan, add the rabbit legs and brown lightly on both sides, then drain on kitchen paper.

2 Heat the butter in a heavy-based saucepan, add the onion and cook gently until soft. Add the flour and stir well. Gradually add the cider, stirring well, then add the chicken stock. Bring to the boil, add the rabbit legs and season lightly with salt and pepper. Cover the pan and simmer gently for 1¼ hours or until the rabbit is tender.

3 Remove the rabbit legs with a slotted spoon and set aside. Add the cream to the cooking liquor and continue to simmer until the sauce has thickened. Put the legs back into the sauce with the parsley and bring back to the boil. Serve with some good mashed potato or a mashed root vegetable.

If wild rabbits are not available, buy tender farmed rabbits instead. These are about twice the size of the wild ones, so one leg is almost enough for one person.

Chicken and ham pie

Serves 4

600ml (1 pint) chicken stock
500g (1lb 2oz) skinless chicken
   thigh fillets
3 large leeks, trimmed, roughly
   chopped and rinsed
40g (1½oz) butter
40g (1½oz) plain flour, plus extra
   to dust
100ml (3½fl oz) double cream
200g (7oz) good quality ham,
   trimmed of fat (preferably home-
   cooked, see page 175)
2 tbsp chopped parsley
350–400g (12–14oz) good quality
   puff pastry
1 medium egg, beaten
sea salt and white pepper

1 Pour the chicken stock into a shallow pan and bring to the boil. Lower the heat, add the chicken thighs and poach gently for 10 minutes. Remove with a slotted spoon and put to one side.

2 Add the leeks to the chicken stock and simmer gently for 10 minutes, then drain in a colander over a bowl to retain the stock.

3 Melt the butter in a heavy-based pan, add the flour and stir well. Gradually add the reserved stock, stirring constantly to avoid lumps. Bring to the boil, season with a little salt and pepper, and simmer gently for about 5 minutes, stirring every so often. Add the cream, bring back to the boil and simmer for a further 5 minutes. The sauce should be quite thick by now; if not, simmer a little longer until it is, then leave to cool.

4 Cut the ham roughly into 2cm (¾ inch) cubes. Add to the cooled sauce with the leeks, chicken and parsley. Adjust the seasoning, then spoon into 4 individual pie dishes, or one large one to 1cm (½ inch) from the top.

5 Roll the puff pastry out on a floured surface to a 5mm (¼ inch) thickness. Cut out top(s) for the pie(s) about 2cm (¾ inch) larger all the way round than the dish(es). Brush the edges of the pastry with a little of the beaten egg. Lay the pastry over the top of the pie dish(es), pressing the egg-washed sides against the rim. Cut a small slit in the top of each pie to allow steam to escape and brush the pastry with beaten egg. Leave to rest in a cool place for 30 minutes.

6 Preheat the oven to 200°C (fan oven 180°C), gas mark 6. Cook the pie(s) for 40–50 minutes until the pastry is golden. Serve hot.

Cock-a-leekie

Serves 4

200g (7oz) piece of stewing beef,
  such as shin or flank
2 litres (3½ pints) chicken stock
200g (7oz) large leeks, halved
  lengthways and rinsed

4 chicken legs, skinned
16 large good quality pitted prunes,
  soaked in warm water overnight
150g (5oz) small finger leeks, halved
  if long and rinsed
sea salt and pepper

1 Put the beef into a saucepan with the chicken stock. Add the large leeks, trimming them to fit the pan if necessary. Bring to the boil and skim off any scum that forms on the surface. Season with salt and pepper, then simmer gently for 1½ hours.

2 Meanwhile, cut the chicken legs in half at the joint, and chop the knuckles off the drumsticks. Add the chicken legs to the pan and simmer for another 30 minutes.

3 Drain though a colander into a bowl and reserve the chicken and beef, discarding the leeks. Skim the stock and strain through a fine sieve into a clean pan. Add the prunes and finger leeks. Cut the beef into 4 pieces and return to the pan with the chicken. Simmer for another 15 minutes until the leeks are tender. Adjust the seasoning, if necessary.

4 Serve the cock-a-leekie as it is or, for a more refined soup, remove the chicken from the bone, shred the meat and return to the soup.

This ancient soupy stew is usually attributed to the Scots but it is also sometimes claimed by the Welsh.

Kentish pudding

Serves 4–6

For the suet pastry

275g (10oz) self-raising flour, plus extra to dust

140g (4½oz) suet

½ tsp salt

For the filling

50g (2oz) butter, plus extra to grease

750g (1lb 10oz) boneless skinless chicken thighs, halved

1 large onion, peeled and finely chopped

100g (3½oz) rindless smoked streaky bacon, cut into 2cm (¾ inch) pieces

250g (9oz) button mushrooms, halved or quartered, depending on size

3 tbsp plain flour, plus extra to dust

4 tbsp white wine

350ml (12fl oz) chicken stock

2 tbsp chopped parsley

sea salt and pepper

1 To make the suet pastry, mix the flour, suet and salt together in a bowl, then mix to a soft dough with about 100ml (3½fl oz) cold water. Roll out to a circle large enough to line a 2 litre (3½ pint) pudding basin. Cut a quarter out of the circle for the lid and to ease the lining of the bowl. Grease the pudding basin well with butter, drop the larger piece of pastry into it and join up the edges where the quarter was removed. Trim the edges around the rim of the bowl.

2 Season the chicken with salt and pepper and flour lightly. Melt 15g (½oz) of the butter in a large frying pan and cook the chicken pieces for a couple of minutes on each side without allowing them to colour (you may need to do this in 2 batches). Remove from the pan and put to one side.

3 Melt the rest of the butter in the pan, add the onion and bacon, and cook gently until the onion is soft, then add the mushrooms and cook for another 2–3 minutes, stirring well, until they soften. Add the flour, stir well, then slowly stir in the wine and stock and bring to the boil, stirring. Remove from the heat and leave to cool.

4 Add the chicken and parsley to the sauce, mix well and adjust the seasoning. Tip the mixture into the lined pudding basin. Remould the pastry for the lid and roll it out to the correct size. Lay it over the filling and press the edges together to seal in the filling, trimming as necessary.

5 Cover the top generously with a piece of pleated foil and secure under the rim with string, making a handle so the pudding basin can be lifted easily. Lower the pudding into a pan containing enough boiling water to come about halfway up the side of the basin. Cover with a lid and simmer very gently for 4 hours, topping up with more boiling water as necessary. Lift the pudding out, remove the foil and serve straight from the basin.

Originally this dish would have been made using a boiling fowl, but boneless chicken thighs are perfect for the long slow cooking as they keep their shape and don't dry out. Vary the mushrooms as you please – girolles, for example, would give a great flavour.

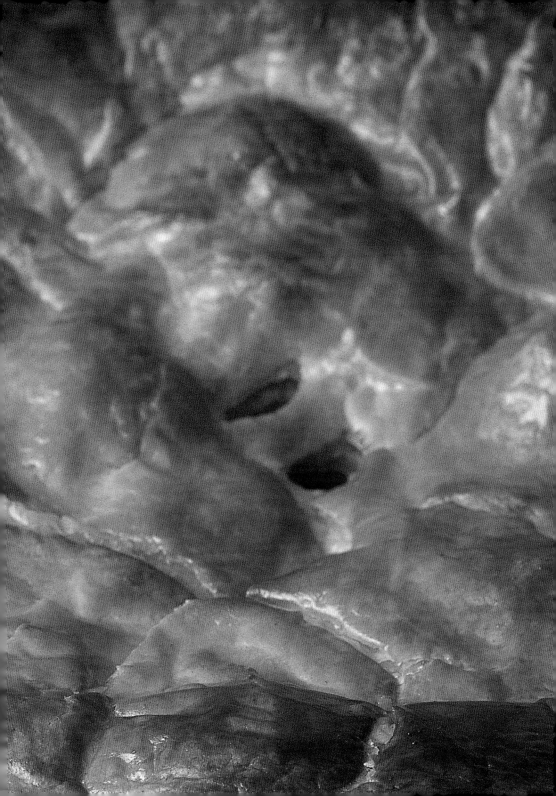

Game pie

Illustrated on previous pages

Serves 4

1kg (2¼lb) boneless game meat, such as leg of venison and game bird thighs

2 glasses of good red wine

1 garlic clove, peeled and crushed

1 tsp chopped thyme

4 juniper berries, crushed

1 bay leaf

2 tbsp vegetable oil

2 tbsp plain flour, plus extra to dust

25g (1oz) butter

1 large onion, peeled and finely chopped

1 tsp tomato purée

1 litre (1¾ pints) beef stock

350–400g (12–14oz) good quality puff pastry

1 medium egg, beaten

sea salt and pepper

1 About 2 days ahead, cut the game roughly into 3cm (1¼ inch) cubes and put into a stainless steel (or other non-reactive) bowl with the red wine, garlic, thyme, juniper berries and bay leaf. Cover with cling film and marinate in the fridge for 2 days.

2 Drain the meat in a colander over a bowl, reserving the marinade, and dry the pieces on kitchen paper. Heat the oil in a large heavy-based frying pan until almost smoking. Meanwhile, lightly flour the meat with ½ tbsp of the flour, seasoned with salt and pepper. Fry the meat in 2 or 3 batches over a high heat until nicely browned, then remove and set aside.

3 Heat the butter in the pan and gently fry the onion until soft. Add the remaining flour and tomato purée and stir over a low heat for a minute. Slowly stir in the marinade and stock. Bring to the boil, then add the meat, cover and simmer gently for 1–2 hours or until the meat is tender. Or cook in the oven at 170°C (fan oven 150°C), gas mark 3. Start checking the meat after 1 hour; it's difficult to put an exact time on braised meats. Once it is cooked, the sauce should have thickened to the consistency of gravy. (If not, thicken with 1–2 tsp cornflour mixed with a little cold water and simmer briefly, stirring.)

4 Allow the game mixture to cool, then use to fill a large pie dish, to 1cm (½ inch) from the rim, discarding the bay leaf.

5 Roll out the pastry on a floured surface to a 5mm (¼ inch) thickness and cut out a round or oval, about 2cm (¾ inch) larger all round than the pie dish. Brush the pastry edges with a little beaten egg. Lay the pastry on top of the dish, pushing the sides against the rim. Cut a small slit in the top to allow steam to escape and brush with beaten egg. Leave to rest in a cool place for 30 minutes. Meanwhile, preheat the oven to 200°C (fan oven 180°C), gas mark 6.

6 Bake the pie for 40–50 minutes until the pastry is crisp and golden.

Game for pies is traditionally a mixture of game birds, rabbit, hare and diced venison. As these take different times to cook, I find the best solution is to use a mixture of game bird thighs and tender cuts from the leg of venison. You'll need to marinate the meat a couple of days in advance.

british
meat

Steak and oyster pie

Serves 4–6

800g (1¾lb) braising beef (flank, skirt or shin)

1 glass of good red wine

150ml (¼ pint) stout

1 garlic clove, peeled and crushed

1 tsp chopped thyme leaves

1 bay leaf

2 tbsp vegetable oil

2 tbsp plain flour, plus extra to dust

25g (1oz) butter

1 small onion, peeled and finely chopped

1 tsp tomato purée

1.5 litres (2½ pints) beef stock

1–2 tsp cornflour, mixed with a little water (optional)

4 or 8 rock oysters, opened and removed from their shells (see page 64)

350–400g (12–14oz) good quality puff pastry

1 medium egg, beaten

sea salt and pepper

1 Cut the beef into 3cm (1¼ inch) cubes and place in a non-reactive bowl with the wine, stout, garlic, thyme and bay leaf. Cover and leave to marinate in the fridge for 2 days.

2 Drain the meat, reserving the marinade, and pat dry. Heat the oil in a heavy-based frying pan. Season ½ tbsp flour and use to lightly coat the meat, then fry the meat in batches over a high heat until browned.

3 Heat the butter in a large heavy-based pan and gently fry the onion until soft. Add the remaining flour and tomato purée, and cook, stirring, for 1 minute. Slowly stir in the marinade, then bring to the boil and reduce by half. Add the stock and beef, then cover and simmer gently for 2–2½ hours, until the meat is tender and the sauce is a gravy-like consistency.

4 If you need to thicken the liquor, stir in the blended cornflour and simmer, stirring, for 1–2 minutes. Allow to cool.

5 Spoon the steak mixture into 4 individual pie dishes, filling them to 1cm (½ inch) from the top. Add 1 or 2 oysters to each dish.

6 Roll out the pastry on a lightly floured surface to a 5mm (¼ inch) thickness and cut out pie lids, 2cm (¾ inch) larger all round than the dishes. Brush the edges with beaten egg and lay the pastry over the filling, pressing the edges on to the rims. Cut a slit in the middle of each lid and brush the pastry with beaten egg. Leave to rest in a cool place for 30 minutes. Preheat the oven to 200°C (fan oven 180°C), gas mark 6.

7 Bake the pies for 40–50 minutes until golden brown. Serve with mash, either plain or flavoured.

Braised beef in Guinness

Serves 4

4 thick-cut pieces of braising beef,
  preferably flank, skirt or shin,
  each about 250–300g (9–11oz) and
  3–4cm (1¼–1½ inches) thick
1 glass of good red wine
150ml (¼ pint) Guinness
1 garlic clove, peeled and crushed
1 tsp chopped thyme leaves
1 bay leaf

1½ tbsp plain flour
2 tbsp vegetable oil
25g (1oz) butter
1 small onion, peeled and finely
  chopped
1 tsp tomato purée
1.2 litres (2 pints) beef stock
1 tsp cornflour (optional)
sea salt and pepper

1 Two days ahead, put the pieces of beef into a stainless steel (or other non-reactive) bowl with the red wine, Guinness, garlic, thyme and bay leaf. Cover with cling film and marinate in the fridge for 2 days.

2 Drain the meat in a colander over a bowl, reserving the marinade, and dry the pieces on kitchen paper. Season ½ tbsp of the flour with salt and pepper and use to lightly flour the meat. Heat the oil in a heavy-based frying pan and fry the meat over a high heat until nicely browned.

3 Heat the butter in a large heavy-based saucepan and gently fry the onion for about 5 minutes until soft. Add the remaining flour and tomato purée, and stir over a low heat for a minute. Slowly add the marinade, stirring constantly to avoid lumps forming. Bring to the boil and simmer until reduced by half.

4 Add the beef stock and the pieces of beef. Bring back to a simmer, cover with a lid and simmer very gently for about 2–2½ hours until the meat is tender. It's difficult to put an exact time on braised meats, sometimes an extra half an hour may be required. The best way to check whether the meat is cooked is by tasting.

5 Once the meat is cooked, the sauce should have thickened to a gravy-like consistency; if not, mix a little cornflour to a paste with some water, stir into the sauce and simmer for a few minutes. Adjust the seasoning if necessary. Serve with colcannon (page 217) or bashed neeps (page 142) to soak up the delicious juices.

Shepherd's pie

Serves 4

450g (1lb) good quality coarse lamb
  mince
450g (1lb) good quality coarse beef
  mince
2 tbsp vegetable oil
500g (1lb 2oz) onions, peeled and
  finely chopped
2 garlic cloves, peeled and crushed
1 tsp chopped thyme leaves
1 tbsp plain flour
1 tbsp tomato purée

1 glass of red wine
1 tbsp Worcestershire sauce
1 litre (1¾ pints) beef stock
sea salt and pepper
For the topping
500g (1lb 2oz) potatoes, peeled and
  quartered
25g (1oz) butter
a little milk
200g (7oz) parsnips, peeled, cored
  and roughly chopped

1 Season the minced meat with salt and pepper. Heat a little oil in a frying
pan until it is almost smoking and cook the meat in small batches for a few
minutes, turning with a wooden spoon, until well coloured, then drain in a
colander to remove the fat.

2 Heat a little more oil in a heavy-based pan and gently fry the onions with
the garlic and thyme until very soft. Add the meat, dust it with the flour and
then add the tomato purée. Cook for a few minutes, stirring constantly.
Slowly stir in the wine, Worcestershire sauce and beef stock. Bring to the
boil, lower the heat and simmer for about 45–50 minutes until the liquid has
thickened. Adjust the seasoning and set aside to cool.

3 Meanwhile, cook the potatoes in boiling salted water for about 15 minutes
until tender. Drain and return to the pan over a low heat for a minute or so
to dry. Mash the potatoes, season well, then add the butter and a dash of
milk to give a firm mash.

4 While the potatoes are cooking, cook the parsnips in boiling salted water
for about 10–12 minutes until they are soft. Drain in a colander, then return
to the pan over a low heat for a minute or so to drive off any excess moisture.
Purée the parsnips in a food processor or mash them smoothly with a potato
masher and mix them with the mashed potato. Season.

5 Preheat the oven to 200°C (fan oven 180°C), gas mark 6. Put the meat into
a large baking dish or individual dishes and top with the potato mixture,
spooning it on evenly and roughing up the surface with a fork. Bake for
35–40 minutes until the topping is golden.

Roast rib eye of beef and Yorkshire pudding

Illustrated on previous pages

Serves 4–6

1 rib-eye of beef off the bone, about
  1–1.5kg (2¼–3¼lb)
beef dripping, or vegetable oil, to
  roast
2 onions, peeled and halved
2 carrots, scrubbed or peeled and
  halved
sea salt and pepper

For the Yorkshire pudding
250g (9oz) plain flour
4 medium eggs, beaten
500–600ml (16fl oz–1 pint) milk
For the gravy
1 glass of red or white wine
200ml (7fl oz) beef stock

1 Preheat the oven to 220°C (fan oven 200°C), gas mark 7. Put a little beef
dripping or oil into a large roasting tin and heat in the oven for 10 minutes.
Season the beef and roast for 15 minutes, then turn it over to seal the meat
and keep the juices in. Put the onions and carrots under the beef to act as a
trivet (or use a steel trivet); this helps the beef to cook evenly and flavours
the gravy. Allow 30 minutes per kg (13 minutes per lb) for rare; add another
10 minutes per kg (4 minutes per lb) for medium; or an extra 20 minutes
per kg (6 minutes per lb) for well done. Baste the meat regularly with the
pan juices.

2 Meanwhile, make the Yorkshire batter. Put the flour into a bowl and add a
good pinch of salt. Mix in the eggs and a little of the milk with a whisk to
form a paste. Mix in the rest of the milk, trying not to beat the batter too
much, to give a thick pouring consistency.

3 About 25 minutes before the beef will be ready, pour some of the hot fat
from the beef into a large roasting tin and heat in the oven for 5 minutes
until smoking. Pour the Yorkshire batter into the roasting tin and bake for
30 minutes until well risen and crisp on the outside.

4 Rest the beef for about 15 minutes before carving. To make the gravy,
deglaze the roasting tin with the wine and add the stock. (If required
thicken with 1–2 tsp cornflour mixed with a little water). Simmer, stirring,
for 1–2 minutes. Serve the beef cut into thick slices, with the Yorkshire
pudding and gravy.

Cornish pasties

Makes 6–8

For the pastry

500g (1lb 2oz) plain flour, plus extra
  to dust
2 tsp salt
125g (4½oz) butter, chilled and diced
125g (4½oz) lard, chilled and diced
a little milk, to mix
1 medium egg, beaten, to seal and
  glaze

For the filling

200g (7oz) swede, peeled
200g (7oz) large potatoes, peeled
250ml (8fl oz) beef stock
500g (1lb 2oz) rump or frying steak
1 tbsp vegetable oil
1 large onion, peeled and finely diced
1 tbsp Worcestershire sauce
1 tsp chopped thyme leaves
sea salt and pepper

1 To make the filling, cut the swede and potatoes roughly into 2cm (¾ inch) pieces and cook separately in boiling salted water until just tender. Drain and leave to cool. Meanwhile, boil the beef stock in a pan to reduce right down to 2–3 tbsp. Trim any fat from the steak, then cut into 5mm (¼ inch) pieces, or coarsely mince.

2 Heat the oil in a large heavy-based pan and gently cook the onion until translucent, then add the meat and cook over a high heat, turning, until evenly browned. Add the reduced stock, Worcestershire sauce, thyme leaves and some seasoning, and cook over a medium heat until the stock has almost totally reduced. Set aside to cool.

3 To make the pastry, mix the flour and salt together, then rub in the butter and lard with your fingers, or using a food processor, until the texture of fine breadcrumbs. Mix in enough milk to give a smooth dough that leaves the sides of the bowl clean.

4 Roll out the pastry on a lightly floured board to a 3mm (⅛ inch) thickness and cut out 6 rounds, about 18cm (7 inches) in diameter, using a plate or bowl as a template.

5 Add the vegetables to the cooled meat, mix well and adjust the seasoning. Spoon the filling evenly along the middle of the pastry discs, then brush around the edges with beaten egg. Bring the edges of the pastry up over the filling and crimp the edges together with your fingers. Brush with egg and cut a small slit in the top for steam to escape. Chill for about 30 minutes. Meanwhile, preheat the oven to 200°C (fan oven 180°C), gas mark 6.

6 Bake the pasties for 20 minutes, then turn the oven down to 180°C (fan oven 160°C), gas mark 4 and cook them for another 20 minutes or so until golden. If the pasties are browning too fast, cover them loosely with foil.

Cornwall's famous pasties were first made for miners, fishermen, farmers and children to take to work or school, though fillings would vary according to their pockets. Some pasties would only contain swede, potato and onion, plus some leek, and perhaps ham off-cuts.

Boiled salt beef with carrots and dumplings

Serves 4

1kg (2¼lb) joint of salted silverside
   or brisket
4 small onions, peeled
12 small carrots, peeled
3 cloves
10 black peppercorns
2 mace blades
1 bay leaf
few thyme sprigs

For the horseradish dumplings

125g (4oz) plain flour, plus extra
   to dust
1 tsp baking powder
½ tsp sea salt
65g (2½oz) suet
1 tbsp chopped parsley
1 tbsp freshly grated horseradish

1 Soak the joint of salt beef in cold water to cover overnight to remove the excess salt.

2 The next day, drain the meat and rinse in cold water, then put into a large saucepan with the onions, carrots, cloves, black peppercorns, mace blades, bay leaf and thyme sprigs. Add enough water to cover the beef by about 6cm (2½ inches) and bring to the boil. Immediately lower the heat and simmer gently, covered, for about 2½–3 hours until tender, removing the carrots and onions as soon as they are cooked; set these aside.

3 In the meantime, make the dumplings. Sift the flour, baking powder and salt into a bowl. Mix in the suet, chopped parsley and grated horseradish, then add enough water to form a sticky dough. Flour your hands and roll the dough into 12 balls.

4 When the beef is cooked, lift it out of the pan and keep warm. Add the dumplings to the cooking liquid and poach for 15 minutes, then remove and keep warm.

5 Strain the liquid through a fine sieve. Return to the pan and boil to reduce by about half, until it has a good strong flavour. Skim off any fat.

6 To serve, reheat the onions, carrots and dumplings in the reduced liquor. Slice the beef and serve in deep plates with the carrots, onions and dumplings, spooning over some of the liquid.

Boiled ham with parsley sauce

Serves 4

4 unsmoked ham hocks, each
   300–400g (11–14oz), or a 1kg
   (2¼lb), boned ham or bacon joint
4 small onions, peeled
2 carrots, peeled and halved
1 bay leaf
3 cloves
few thyme sprigs
1 tsp black peppercorns

For the parsley sauce

25g (1oz) butter
2 shallots, peeled and finely chopped
25g (1oz) plain flour
1 tsp English mustard
150ml (¼ pint) milk
2 tbsp double cream
2 tbsp chopped parsley
sea salt and pepper

1 Soak the ham hocks, or ham or bacon joint in water to cover overnight to remove the excess salt.

2 The next day, drain the meat and rinse in cold water, then put into a large saucepan with the onions, carrots, bay leaf, cloves, thyme sprigs and black peppercorns. Cover with cold water and bring to the boil, then immediately lower the heat and simmer for 3 hours.

3 Towards the end of the cooking time, make the parsley sauce. Melt the butter in a heavy-based pan, add the shallots and cook gently until soft. Add the flour and mustard, stirring well. Gradually stir in the milk and 150ml (¼ pint) of the ham cooking liquid. Bring to the boil and simmer for about 20 minutes until quite thick, stirring occasionally. Add the cream and chopped parsley, adjust the seasoning and simmer for another minute.

4 When the ham is cooked, remove from the pan and leave until cool enough to handle. Remove and discard the fat from the hocks, then carefully remove the outer section of meat and the large bone, leaving the small bone attached to the central eye of meat. Alternatively, if you are using a ham joint, just remove the string and carve into thick slices. Serve with the parsley sauce and accompany with mash or colcannon (page 217).

Enjoy a tasty, hot home-cooked ham and use leftovers cold for sandwiches and salads.

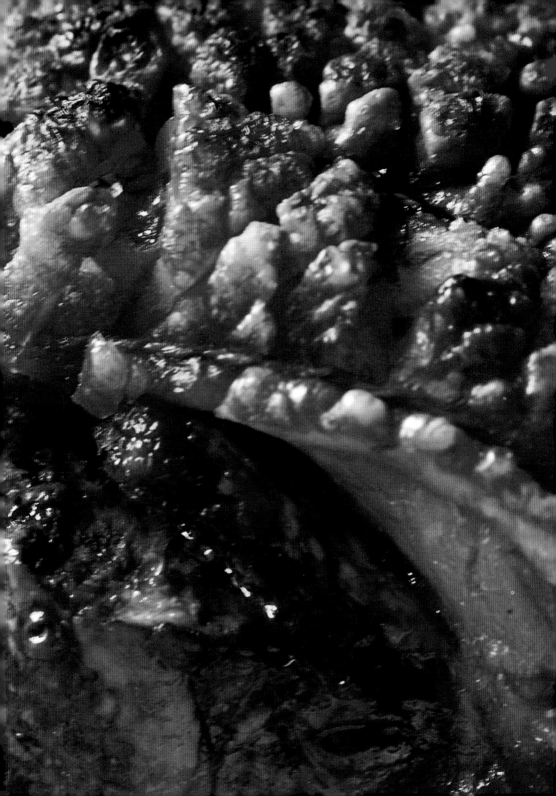

Roast pork with Bramley apple sauce

Illustrated on previous pages

Serves 4–6
1 boned and rolled joint of pork,
  about 1–1.5kg (2¼–3¼lb)
olive oil, to brush
1–2 onions, peeled and cut into
  chunks
3–4 carrots, peeled and cut into
  chunks
sea salt

For the gravy
½ tbsp plain flour
½ glass of red or white wine
500ml (16fl oz) beef stock
For the Bramley apple sauce
good knob of butter
650g (1lb 7oz) Bramley apples,
  peeled, cored and cut into chunks
50g (2oz) light brown sugar, or to
  taste

1 If it hasn't been done already, score the skin of the joint with a very sharp knife at about 5mm–1cm (¼–½ inch) intervals, cutting right through to the fat. Rub some sea salt and olive oil over the skin and leave to stand at room temperature for about 45 minutes. Alternatively, you can pour boiling water over the skin, which scalds it and helps to crisp it up, then proceed as above.
2 Preheat the oven to 200°C (fan oven 180°C), gas mark 6. Heat a roasting tin in the oven, then add the pork with the onions and carrots. Roast in the oven for about 1½ hours, basting the joint every so often. If the pork appears to be browning too rapidly, the oven may need to be turned down slightly.
3 When the pork is cooked through, remove it from the roasting tin and leave to rest on a plate. Don't be tempted to cover the pork with foil as the steam will make the crackling go soft (the crackling itself functions like a cover and keeps the heat in the meat). If the crackling isn't crisp, you can always cut it from the meat and finish it in the oven.

4 For the gravy, dust the vegetables in the roasting tin with the flour and cook over a low heat on the hob for 2 minutes. Add the wine and stock, and simmer for a few minutes, scraping up any residue from the bottom of the tin with a wooden spoon. Transfer everything to a saucepan and simmer for 20 minutes.

5 Meanwhile, make the apple sauce. Melt the butter in a frying pan and sauté the apples with one third of the sugar for about 5 minutes until nicely coloured and beginning to break down. Continuing to stir, add the rest of the sugar (to taste) and cook for a few more minutes until the apples are broken down but not completely puréed.

6 Strain the gravy through a fine sieve into a jug. To serve, slice the pork through the crackling. Pour some hot gravy over each plateful of meat and serve the rest on the side, with the apple sauce.

Getting the crackling on roast pork right isn't as difficult as people think. Although getting the cooking of the pork right in conjunction with crisp crackling can be tricky, especially with smaller cuts. I find a boned and rolled leg joint works well, and it has a good flavour.

Barnsley chops with shallots and parsley

Serves 4

500g (1lb 2oz) shallots, unpeeled
4 Barnsley chops (see below), each
   about 200g (7oz)
100ml (3½fl oz) lamb or beef stock
good knob of unsalted butter
1 tbsp chopped parsley
sea salt and pepper

1 Preheat the oven to 200°C (fan oven 180°C), gas mark 6. Put the shallots, still in their skins, in a roasting tin and bake for 45 minutes. Leave them to cool, then top and tail them with a sharp knife and gently squeeze the onions out their skins.
2 When the shallots are almost cooked, heat a lightly oiled griddle pan or the grill to its hottest setting. Season the chops with salt and pepper, and grill for 4–5 minutes on each side for pink, or 7–8 minutes for medium.
3 While the chops are cooking, put the shallots into a frying pan with the stock and cook over a high heat to reduce the stock until it is almost totally evaporated. Add the butter and chopped parsley, lightly season with salt and pepper, and stir until the butter has melted into the liquid to form a glaze.
4 Place the chops on warm plates. Spoon the glazed shallots on top, or serve them separately.

The Barnsley chop is a double loin chop cut across the saddle. If you can't find Barnsley chops, just use two good ordinary loin chops per person.

Roast lamb with mint jelly and lavender

Illustrated on previous pages

Serves 4

2 best ends (racks) of lamb, French
    trimmed, each 400–450g
    (14oz–1lb)
few sprigs of lavender
1 garlic clove, peeled and thinly
    sliced
1 tbsp vegetable oil
sea salt and pepper
pan gravy (page 127), optional, to
    serve

For the mint jelly

2kg (4½lb) cooking apples
300ml (½ pint) cider vinegar
25g (1oz) mint leaves
about 300g (11oz) preserving or
    granulated sugar
10 sheets leaf gelatine

1 Make the mint jelly at least 2 days ahead. Roughly chop the apples, including the peel and cores. Place in a heavy-based saucepan with 1 litre (1¾ pints) water, bring to the boil and simmer very gently for 40 minutes. Add the vinegar and continue cooking for 5 minutes. You'll need a jelly bag and stand, or a stainless steel or plastic colander lined with 3 layers of muslin and set over a bowl. Tip the contents of the pan into the jelly bag or lined colander and allow to drip through for about 4 hours or overnight.

2 Bring a small pan of water to the boil and dip the mint leaves in for 2 seconds only. Drain in a sieve, refresh under cold running water, then dry on kitchen paper. Finely chop the leaves and put to one side.

3 Measure the apple liquid and add 100g (3½oz) sugar for every 100ml (3½fl oz). Pour the liquid into a saucepan, add the sugar and stir over a low heat until dissolved. Bring to the boil and boil for 5 minutes. Meanwhile, soak the gelatine leaves in cold water to cover for a few minutes to soften, then squeeze out the excess liquid. Remove the apple syrup from the heat, add the gelatine, stirring to dissolve, then stir in the mint. Pour into sterilised Kilner jars, seal and store in a cool dark place, or refrigerate.

4 When ready to cook the lamb, preheat the oven to 220°C (fan oven 200°C), gas mark 7. With a small sharp knife, make 8–10 incisions in the fat covering the lamb, about 1cm (½ inch) deep. Put a tiny sprig of lavender and a slice of garlic into each slit and season the lamb with salt and pepper.

5 Spoon the oil into a shallow roasting tin and heat in the oven for about 5 minutes. Put the lamb racks in the roasting tin, fat side down, and roast for 15 minutes, then turn the lamb over and cook for another 15 minutes for pink meat; roast for another 10 minutes for medium; or an extra 15 minutes for well done meat.

6 Transfer the lamb to a warmed plate and leave to rest in a warm place for 5 minutes while you make a gravy with the pan juices. Carve the lamb in between the bones and serve with the mint jelly and gravy.

Lavender, like rosemary, gives an amazing aroma to lamb as it roasts and fresh mint jelly is the perfect partner. You'll have more mint jelly than you need here, but it will keep for a few months in the fridge in sterilised jars.

Irish stew

Serves 4–6
600–700g (1¼–1½lb) lamb neck fillet
1 litre (1¾ pints) lamb stock
1 tsp chopped thyme leaves
500g (1lb 2oz) large button onions,
   or small onions about the size of a
   squash ball, peeled
700g (1½lb) small baking potatoes,
   or large new potatoes (same size as
   onions), peeled
sea salt and pepper

1 Cut the lamb into 4cm (1½ inch) chunks and put into a heavy-based pan with the stock and thyme leaves. Season with salt and pepper and bring to the boil. Lower the heat and simmer for 30 minutes.

2 Add the onions to the pan and simmer for another 20 minutes. Meanwhile, preheat the oven to 180°C (fan oven 160°C), gas mark 4.

3 Transfer the contents of the pan to an ovenproof dish, stir in the potatoes and cover with a lid. Cook in the oven for 1 hour or a little longer if the lamb is not soft. Depending on the time of year, the lamb can be a little tougher and will take more cooking.

There is much discussion about the correct ingredients for an Irish stew. Mutton neck chops are traditional, but lamb neck fillet is more readily available these days and remains moist during long cooking, giving the broth the perfect depth of natural flavour.

Leg of lamb with caper sauce

Serves 4

1 boned and rolled leg of lamb, about
   800g–1kg (1¾–2¼lb)
2 onions, peeled and halved
1 leek, trimmed, roughly chopped
   and rinsed
few thyme sprigs
1 bay leaf
10 black peppercorns
600ml (1 pint) chicken stock
1 tsp salt

For the caper sauce

25g (1oz) butter
25g (1oz) plain flour
100ml (3½fl oz) double cream
100g (3½oz) capers, rinsed in cold
   water
1 tbsp chopped parsley
sea salt and pepper

1 Put the lamb into a saucepan into which it just fits and add the onions,
leek, thyme, bay leaf and peppercorns. Mix the chicken stock with an equal
quantity of water and pour into the pan to cover the meat. (If necessary, add
a little more water or dilute stock). Add the salt and bring to the boil. Skim
off any scum from the surface, lower the heat and simmer for 1½ hours.
Pour 500ml (16fl oz) of the stock into a jug (for the sauce) and leave the
lamb in the rest of the liquor, covered with a lid, until required.

2 To make the sauce, melt the butter in a heavy-based pan, add the flour and
stir well. Gradually stir in the reserved stock and bring to the boil. Remove
the cooked onions from the lamb cooking liquor and add them to the sauce.
Simmer for 30 minutes over a low heat.

3 Transfer the sauce to a blender or food processor and whiz until smooth,
then pass through a fine sieve into a clean pan. Add the cream and simmer
until the sauce has thickened to a coating consistency. Add the capers and
parsley, and season with salt and pepper to taste.

4 Remove the lamb from the cooking liquid and place on a board. Remove
any string and cut the lamb into 5mm–1cm (¼–½ inch) thick slices. Arrange
on warm plates and serve with the caper sauce.

Lancashire hot pot

Illustrated on previous pages

Serves 4

800g (1¾lb) lamb neck fillet
flour, to dust
6 lambs' kidneys, halved and
    trimmed (optional)
4–5 tbsp vegetable oil
500g (1lb 2oz) onions, peeled and
    thinly sliced

65g (2½oz) unsalted butter, plus
    extra to brush
800ml (1⅓ pints) lamb or beef stock
1 tsp chopped rosemary leaves
1 kg (2¼lb) large potatoes, peeled
    and thinly sliced
sea salt and pepper

1 Preheat the oven to 220°C (fan oven 200°C), gas mark 7. Cut the lamb roughly into 3–4cm (1¼–1½ inch) chunks, season with salt and pepper and dust with flour. Season and lightly flour the kidneys if using, keeping them separate from the meat.

2 Heat 2 tbsp oil in a heavy-based frying pan and fry the lamb, a few pieces at a time, over a high heat until they are nicely coloured. Drain in a colander. Fry and drain the kidneys in the same way, then mix with the lamb and set aside.

3 Wipe the pan clean. Heat another 2 tbsp oil in the pan and fry the onions over a high heat until they begin to colour. Add the butter and continue to cook for a few minutes until the onions soften. Dust them with 1 tbsp of flour, stir well, then gradually add the stock, stirring to avoid lumps. Sprinkle in the chopped rosemary. Bring to the boil, season with salt and pepper and simmer for about 10 minutes.

4 Now you're ready to assemble the pot. Cover the bottom of a casserole dish with a layer of potatoes, then add a layer of meat with a little sauce, then another layer of potatoes. Continue until the meat has all been used. Finish the top with a layer of nicely overlapping potato slices.

5 Brush the top layer of potatoes with a little of the sauce. Cover and cook in the oven for about 30 minutes, then turn the oven down to 140°C (fan oven 120°C), gas mark 1 and cook for a further 2 hours.

6 Remove the lid from the pot and turn the oven back up to 220°C (fan oven 200°C), gas mark 7. Brush the top with a little melted butter and cook, uncovered, for a further 15–20 minutes to brown the potatoes.

Devilled lambs' kidneys

Serves 4

20 lambs' kidneys, halved and
  trimmed of sinews
1–2 tbsp vegetable oil
good knob of butter
3 shallots, peeled and finely chopped
1 garlic clove, peeled and crushed
2 tbsp cider vinegar

2 tsp English mustard
2 tsp tomato ketchup
100ml (3½fl oz) pan gravy (page
  127), or basic gravy (page 132)
1 tbsp chopped parsley
sea salt and cayenne pepper
4 thick slices of buttered toast,
  to serve

1 Heat a frying pan until almost smoking. Season the kidneys with salt and
cayenne pepper and fry them in a little oil for 2 minutes over a high heat
until coloured but still pink. Transfer them to a plate.

2 Melt the butter in a saucepan, add the shallots and garlic, and cook gently
for a couple of minutes until soft. Add the cider vinegar, mustard and
ketchup, and simmer for a minute. Add the gravy and parsley, bring to the
boil and simmer for a couple of minutes until the sauce is thick.

3 Add the kidneys to the pan and simmer for 30 seconds to reheat them.
Spoon on to hot buttered toast and serve straightaway.

This makes a good breakfast or brunch dish,
or you can serve it as a light main course.
Always try to buy fresh lambs' kidneys, as
they will have a better texture when cooked
than frozen ones.

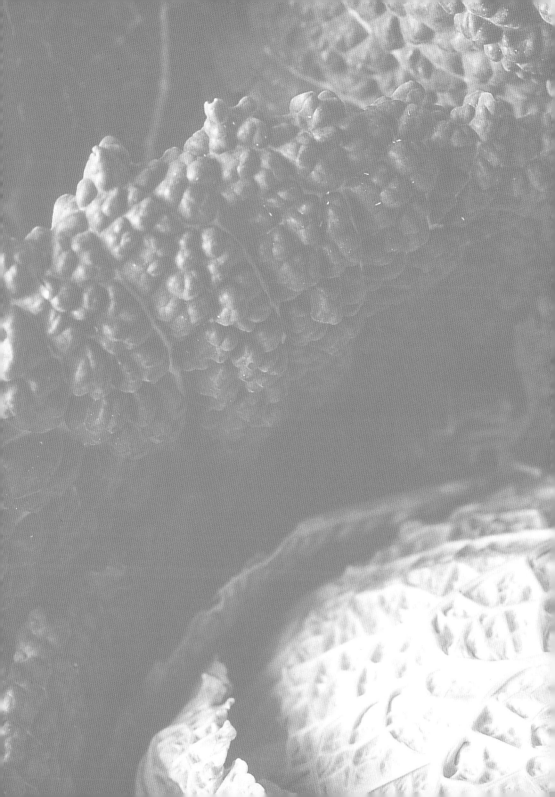

british
vegetables

Buttered greens with cob nuts

Serves 4

1kg (2¼lb) spring greens or Savoy
   cabbage, trimmed and stalk
   removed
100g (3½oz) shelled cob nuts
65g (2½oz) butter
sea salt and pepper

1 Cut the spring greens or cabbage roughly into 3cm (1¼ inch) squares.
Cook in plenty of boiling salted water for 4–5 minutes until tender, then
drain in a colander.
2 Meanwhile, preheat the grill to medium. Roughly chop the cob nuts and
toast lightly. Drain the greens well and toss with the toasted nuts and butter.
Season with salt and pepper, then serve.

Kentish cob nuts are available during the
autumn months and they lend a nice texture
to greens. If you've missed the cob nut season,
then chestnuts make a good alternative.

Buttered samphire

Serves 4
300–400g (11–14oz) samphire,
  woody stalks trimmed
melted butter (as much as you like)
freshly ground black pepper

1 Cook the samphire in boiling unsalted water (or steam it if you prefer) for
2–3 minutes until tender. Drain thoroughly in a colander.
2 Toss the samphire with melted butter and black pepper to taste, then serve
straightaway.

Marsh samphire, or sea asparagus, can be
found on the salt marshes around the coast
during the summer months. It has a natural
salty taste of the sea, which makes it a perfect
accompaniment for fish.

Peas with bacon and onions

Serves 4

125g (4oz) slices of rindless streaky
  bacon

75g (3oz) butter

400g (14oz) shelled fresh or frozen
  peas

2 tsp sugar

1 bunch of spring onions
  (preferably bulbous ones)

sea salt and pepper

1 Cut the bacon into 1cm (½ inch) dice. Melt 25g (1oz) butter in a pan and gently cook the bacon over a low heat for 3–4 minutes without allowing it to colour.

2 Meanwhile, put the peas into a saucepan and add enough boiling water to just cover them. Add 25g (1oz) of the remaining butter, season well and add the sugar. Bring back to the boil and cook over a medium heat for 5 minutes (2 minutes only for frozen) or until tender. Drain in a colander set over a bowl to save the liquid.

3 Cut the spring onions into 2.5cm (1 inch) lengths, put into the empty pan and pour just enough of the reserved liquid over to cover them. Boil rapidly until most of the liquid has evaporated, then add the rest of the butter and mix with the peas and the bacon. Check the seasoning and serve.

Bacon and spring onions give peas a new lease of life. Use fresh peas when they are in season – you'll need about 1kg (2¼lb) peas in the pod to give this shelled weight.

Creamed Brussels sprouts

Serves 4–6
500g (1lb 2oz) large Brussels
   sprouts
150ml (¼ pint) double cream
50g (2oz) butter
sea salt and pepper

1 Cook the sprouts in boiling salted water for 5–10 minutes until just tender, then drain well and allow to cool slightly. Slice the sprouts thinly.
2 Boil the cream to reduce by half, then add the sprouts and season with salt and pepper. Simmer for 4–5 minutes over a low heat, stirring every so often. Add the butter and serve.

This is a good way to use up leftover Brussels sprouts, or you can prepare them from fresh. Serve to accompany poultry and game dishes.

Turnips with chervil

Serves 4
800g (1¾lb) young turnips, peeled
2 tsp sugar
100g (3½oz) butter
1 tbsp chopped chervil
sea salt and pepper

1 If the turnips are very small leave them whole, otherwise quarter them. Put them into a pan and just cover with boiling water. Add the sugar and half of the butter, and season generously with salt and pepper. Bring back to the boil and cook over a medium heat for 7–8 minutes or until the turnips are tender.
2 Drain the turnips in a colander, then toss with the remaining butter and chopped chervil. Taste and adjust the seasoning, then serve.

Prepared and cooked in the right way, turnips, swede and parsnips are the best of the root vegetables. I find it odd that they are dismissed as cattle fodder by some, especially in France.

Roasted marrow with garlic and herbs

Serves 4
1 young marrow, about 1kg (2¼lb)
1 tbsp olive oil
2 tsp chopped thyme leaves
4 garlic cloves, peeled and crushed
65g (2½oz) butter
2 tbsp chopped parsley
sea salt and pepper

1 Cut the marrow into quarters lengthways and scoop out the seeds with a spoon. Cut the flesh into 2cm (¾ inch) thick slices, lay them on a tray and season well with salt and pepper. Leave to stand for 30 minutes. Preheat the oven to 230°C (fan oven 210°C), gas mark 8.

2 Heat the olive oil in a roasting tray in the oven for 5 minutes. Add the marrow slices and sprinkle with the chopped thyme. Roast for 15 minutes, turning occasionally, then add the crushed garlic and cook for a further 5–10 minutes until the marrow is nicely browned.

3 To serve, toss the roasted marrow with the butter and chopped parsley.

Try to choose young marrows, as these have the best flavour and their skin can be left on.

Roasted beets with horseradish

Illustrated on previous pages

Serves 4
1kg (2¼lb) small beetroot
1–2 tbsp olive oil
few thyme sprigs
65g (2½oz) freshly grated
   horseradish
knob of butter
sea salt and pepper

1 Cook the beetroot in their skins in a pan of boiling salted water for about
1 hour or until they are tender to the point of a knife. Drain in a colander
and leave to cool. Preheat the oven to 200°C (fan oven 180°C), gas mark 6.
2 Wearing rubber gloves to avoid staining your hands, remove the skin from
the beetroot and trim the ends if necessary. If the beetroot are very small
leave them whole, otherwise cut into quarters.
3 Heat the olive oil in a roasting tray in the oven for about 5 minutes. Add
the beetroot and season with salt and pepper. Cook for 30 minutes, then
scatter over the thyme and continue cooking for another 15–20 minutes
until nicely coloured.
4 Scatter the horseradish over the beetroot, add the butter and turn to coat,
then return to the oven for 10 minutes. Serve hot.

Fresh beetroot makes a delicious soup, is good in salads and can be cooked simply to serve as an accompaniment. It is an easy vegetable to cook, although a bit messy to peel. If you can't get a hold of fresh horseradish, then the grated horseradish sold in jars works well.

Simple mash

Serves 4
1kg (2¼lb) floury potatoes, peeled
   and quartered
50g (2oz) butter
a little milk or double cream
sea salt and pepper

1 Put the potatoes in a saucepan, cover with cold water and add salt. Bring to the boil and simmer for about 15 minutes until tender. Drain the potatoes and return to the pan over a low heat for a minute or so to dry out.
2 Push the potatoes through a potato ricer into a warm bowl, or mash them in the pan using a hand-held potato masher. Season generously, add the butter and mix well. Stir in a little milk or double cream to taste and check the seasoning.

Note Don't add too much milk or cream, or you will lose the earthy potato taste. Well flavoured potatoes need just a touch of milk, and you certainly won't need cream if you are serving the mash with something as rich as braised beef or duck.

Choosing a potato with a good flavour and texture for mashing can be difficult with so many varieties available, but King Edward is a good all-rounder. A potato ricer is an invaluable tool, as it gets the potatoes nice and fine before you add the butter.

Bubble and squeak

Serves 4–6

150g (5oz cooked swede, chopped
250g (9oz) cooked cabbage, chopped
250g (9oz) cooked Brussels sprouts,
  chopped
1 cooked leek, chopped
250g (9oz) cooked Charlotte or other
  waxy potatoes, quartered

celery salt, to taste
dash of Worcestershire sauce, to
  taste
sea salt and pepper
vegetable oil, for frying
plain flour, to dust

1 Combine the cooked swede, cabbage, Brussels sprouts, leek and potatoes in a bowl and mix well. Flavour with celery salt, Worcestershire sauce and seasoning to taste.

2 Heat a little oil in a non-stick frying pan until almost smoking and fry the mixture a little at a time, turning, until it begins to colour. Then return to the bowl and leave to cool. Adjust the seasoning, mould the cooled mixture into even-sized cakes and refrigerate.

3 When ready to serve, lightly flour the cakes and fry in a little oil for about 3–4 minutes on each side until golden brown. Drain on kitchen paper and serve piping hot.

Bubble and squeak is traditionally made with leftovers but, of course, you can use freshly cooked vegetables. Serve as an accompaniment or topped with a fried egg for brunch.

Colcannon

Serves 4–6

1kg (2¼lb) floury potatoes, peeled
   and quartered
350g (12oz) cabbage, such as Savoy
1 large bunch of spring onions,
   trimmed
50g (2oz) butter
a little milk or double cream
sea salt and pepper

1 Put the potatoes in a saucepan, cover with cold water and add salt. Bring
to the boil and simmer for about 15 minutes until tender. Drain the potatoes
and return to the pan over a low heat for a minute or so to dry out.
2 Meanwhile, cook the cabbage in boiling salted water until tender; drain
well and chop. Blanch the spring onions briefly in boiling water to soften,
then drain and chop finely.
3 Push the potatoes through a potato ricer into a warm bowl, or mash them
in the pan using a hand-held potato masher. Season generously, add the
butter and mix well. Stir in a little milk or double cream to taste and mix in
the spring onions and cabbage. Serve piping hot.

Colcannon is a perfect match for rich stews
and boiled meats. It originates from Ireland,
like its cousin, champ, which is flavoured with
blanched spring onions but not cabbage.

Honey-roasted parsnips

Serves 4–6
700–800g (1½–1¾lb) parsnips
65–75g (2½–3oz) beef dripping
2 tbsp thin honey
sea salt and pepper

1 Top and tail the parsnips. If the skins are clean they don't need to be peeled, otherwise peel them. Quarter the parsnips lengthways and remove the hard core which runs down the centre. Cook the parsnip quarters in boiling salted water for 5 minutes, drain in a colander and leave to cool.
2 Preheat the oven to 200°C (fan oven 180°C), gas mark 6 and heat a roasting tray in the oven. Melt the beef dripping in the hot tray, then add the parsnips and season with salt and pepper. Roast for about 30 minutes, turning occasionally, until the parsnips are nicely coloured. (Alternatively, they can be roasted around a joint of meat.)
3 Add the honey, turn the parsnips to coat and return the tray to the oven for a further 5 minutes, basting once or twice with the honey and dripping until they are golden. Serve immediately.

This is the perfect accompaniment to a roast. Lots of people don't like parsnips for some reason. What a shame – they have a delicious natural fluffy texture and sweet flavour.

This dish seems to appear in different guises all over the world – in France, Wales, even in Spain. An ovenproof frying pan is useful here, otherwise use a non-stick pan and transfer the potato cake to a baking tray to finish cooking in the oven.

Potatoes roasted in goose fat

Serves 4

1.5kg (3¼lb) King Edward or similar
   potatoes, peeled and halved or
   quartered if large
150g (5oz) goose or duck fat
sea salt and pepper

1 Par-cook the potatoes in boiling salted water for 10 minutes. Drain and return to the pan over a low heat for a minute or so to drive off excess moisture. Turn off the heat, put the lid on and leave for 5 minutes, then give the pan a brief shake and leave them for another 15 minutes. This will steam the potatoes through and rough up the edges a bit, which gives them that nice crisp skin and allows the goose fat to be absorbed by the potato. Preheat the oven to 220°C (fan oven 200°C), gas mark 7.

2 Put the goose fat in a roasting tray and preheat in the oven. Season the potatoes with salt and pepper, then add to the tray and roll them in the hot goose fat. Roast for about 45 minutes until crisp, basting every 15 minutes or so. Serve straightaway.

Goose fat gives roast potatoes that rich luxury taste. If you can't find goose or duck fat, then bought or leftover beef dripping from a roast meat joint will give you a close result.

Pease pudding

Serves 4

450g (1lb) dried yellow split peas
about 1 litre (1¾ pints) ham stock
   (see page 175) or chicken stock
1 medium egg, beaten
65g (2½oz) butter, plus extra to
   grease
sea salt and pepper

1 Put the dried split peas in a bowl, cover with cold water and soak overnight.
2 Drain and rinse the soaked split peas, then place in a large pan. Add
enough ham or chicken stock to cover them generously and simmer for
1 hour or so until tender. Drain and tip into a large bowl.
3 Add the egg and butter to the peas and mix well, seasoning with salt and
pepper. Transfer to a greased 1.2 litre (2 pint) pudding basin and cover the
top with a sheet of foil, pleated in the centre to allow room for expansion.
Secure under the rim with string.
4 Put the pudding basin into a steamer or saucepan containing enough
boiling water to come halfway up the side of the basin and steam for 1 hour.
Check the water level during cooking as you may have to top it up with
more boiling water. Alternatively, you can cook it in a deep-roasting tin
half-filled with boiling water in the oven at 180°C (fan oven 160°C), gas
mark 4 for 1 hour.
5 Lift the pudding basin from the pan, remove the foil and run a knife round
the side of the pudding to loosen it. Turn out on to a warm plate and serve.

Traditionally this is made by tying the dried
split peas in muslin and boiling them with a
ham joint. If you've boiled a ham (page 175),
don't discard the stock – use it here, or cook
the two together. Flake pieces of cooked ham
into the pudding for a bit of added texture.

british puddings

Rhubarb syllabub

Serves 4

250g (9oz) young rhubarb, trimmed
  and cut into 2cm (¾ inch) pieces
150g (5oz) caster sugar
3 tbsp grenadine syrup

For the syllabub

400ml (14fl oz) double cream
100g (3½oz) caster sugar
juice of 1 small lemon
1 small glass of sherry or sweet wine

1 Cook the rhubarb with the sugar and grenadine in a covered pan over a medium heat, stirring occasionally, until soft, about 10 minutes. Tip into a strainer set over a bowl, then return the juice to the pan and simmer until reduced by half and thickened. Stir back into the rhubarb and leave to cool.

2 To make the syllabub, mix together the double cream, sugar, lemon juice and sherry. Using an electric mixer or by hand, whip the mixture until standing in soft peaks, then spoon into glasses and chill for an hour or so. To serve, spoon the rhubarb on top.

Rhubarb is available from early February for a few months, but you can use other fruits in season, such as raspberries, plums and exotic fruits, like passion fruit.

Burnt cream

Also illustrated on previous pages

Serves 4
600ml (1 pint) thick Jersey cream
8 medium egg yolks
75g (3oz) caster sugar

1 The day before serving, bring the cream to the boil and reduce by one third. Meanwhile, mix the egg yolks with 1 tbsp of the caster sugar.
2 Pour the reduced cream on to the egg yolks and mix well, then return the mixture to the pan. Cook over a low heat, stirring constantly until the mixture coats the back of a spoon. Don't allow it to boil, or it will curdle. Remove from the heat.
3 Pour the mixture into 4 individual heatproof dishes, such as ramekins, and leave to cool. Chill overnight in the fridge.
4 An hour before serving, sprinkle an even layer of caster sugar over the cream and caramelise under a preheated hot grill or using a blow-torch. Allow to cool and set, then serve as soon as possible.

Whether this dessert is of French or British origin is a matter of debate. There are lots of variations but, like most successful dishes, the simplest ones seem to work the best.

Gooseberry fool

Serves 4

150g (5oz) gooseberries, topped and
  tailed
90g (3½oz) caster sugar, or more to
  sweeten the fruit if needed
5 tbsp dessert wine
juice of ¼ lemon
250ml (8fl oz) double cream

1 Put the gooseberries, 50g (2oz) sugar and 2 tbsp water into a pan and cook
gently over a low heat for 10 minutes, to a jam-like consistency, Adjust the
sweetness, then leave to cool.
2 Mix the wine, lemon juice and remaining 40g (1½oz) sugar together in a
bowl, then add the cream and whip the mixture slowly until standing in soft
peaks, using a whisk or an electric mixer.
3 Fold in three quarters of the gooseberry compote, spoon into glasses and
chill for 1–2 hours. Top with the rest of the fruit to serve.

You can make this fool with other seasonal
fruits, such as strawberries or raspberries, as
well as plums. Sweet, soft fruits that don't
need to be cooked can simply be mashed and
folded through the whipped cream.

Easy fruit jelly

Serves 4

600ml (1 pint) bought or freshly
   pressed raspberry or strawberry
   juice
juice of ½ lemon
about 200g (7oz) caster sugar
5 sheets leaf gelatine

1 Put the raspberry or strawberry juice and the lemon juice in a saucepan
and bring to the boil. Add the caster sugar (you may need more or less
depending on the sweetness of the fruit juice) and stir until dissolved. Bring
to the boil, then remove from the heat.
2 Soak the gelatine leaves in a shallow bowl of cold water for a minute or so
until soft. Squeeze out the excess water, then add the gelatine sheets to the
fruit syrup and stir until dissolved.
3 Pour the jellied fruit syrup into 4 individual jelly moulds or one large one
and chill to set.
4 To turn out, fill a bowl with almost boiling water, dip the moulds in briefly,
then remove and loosen the jelly from the edge slightly with your fingertips.
Turn the moulds over on to plates and carefully unmould.

This fruit jelly is deceptively simple to make
and you can prepare it a day ahead. To give
your jelly a kick, add a generous dash of
kirsch, cassis or an appropriate fruit liqueur.

Elderflower jelly

Serves 4

150ml (¼ pint) Sauternes or other
   good dessert wine
juice of ½ lemon
about 200g (7oz) caster sugar
6 freshly picked elderflower heads,
   or 3 tbsp elderflower cordial
5 sheets leaf gelatine

1 Put the Sauternes or other wine in a saucepan with 400ml (14fl oz) water
and the lemon juice, and bring to the boil. Add the caster sugar and stir
until dissolved. Bring to the boil and remove from the heat.
2 If using the elderflower heads, rinse, pat dry and add them to the warm
syrup, then leave to infuse overnight. The next day, bring the syrup to the
boil again, then strain through a fine-meshed sieve into a bowl.
3 Soak the gelatine leaves in a shallow bowl of cold water for a minute or so
until soft. Squeeze out the excess water, then add the gelatine sheets to the
hot fruit syrup and stir until dissolved. If using elderflower cordial, add it at
this stage.
4 Pour the jelly into a glass serving bowl and chill in the fridge until set.

This is a wonderfully fragrant jelly to make
when elderflowers are in blossom. At other
times you can use elderflower cordial.

Elderflower jelly with summer fruits

Serves 4

150ml (¼ pint) Sauternes or other
  good dessert wine
juice of ½ lemon
about 200g (7oz) caster sugar
6 freshly picked elderflower heads,
  or 3 tbsp elderflower cordial

5 sheets leaf gelatine
150g (5oz) mixed summer fruits
  (raspberries, blueberries, halved
  strawberries, etc)

1 Put the Sauternes or other wine in a saucepan with 400ml (14fl oz) water
and the lemon juice, and bring to the boil. Add the caster sugar and stir
until dissolved. Bring to the boil and remove from the heat.

2 If using the elderflower heads, rinse, pat dry and add them to the warm
syrup, then leave to infuse overnight. The next day, bring the syrup to the
boil again, then strain through a fine-meshed sieve into a bowl.

3 Soak the gelatine leaves in a shallow bowl of cold water for a minute or so
until soft. Squeeze out the excess water, then add the gelatine sheets to the
hot fruit syrup and stir until dissolved. If using elderflower cordial, add it at
this stage.

4 Pour the jelly into a bowl and leave to cool but don't let it set. Combine the
berries and divide half of them between 4 glasses, then pour in half the
cooled, liquid jelly. Chill for an hour or so to set.

5 Top up with the remaining fruits and liquid jelly and chill until set. Serve
with a little pouring cream if you like.

This is an ideal way to serve home-grown
summer berries. Setting the fruits in two
layers keeps them suspended in the jelly so
they don't all float to the top.

Eton mess with strawberries

Serves 4
200g (7oz) ripe strawberries, hulled
100g (3½oz) caster sugar
500ml (16fl oz) double cream
few drops of vanilla extract

For the meringue
1 medium egg white
65g (2½oz) caster sugar

1 To make the meringue, in a clean bowl, whisk the egg white until stiff, then gradually whisk in the caster sugar until the meringue holds firm peaks when the whisk is lifted (use an electric mixer for best results).
2 Spread the meringue in an even layer, about 2 cm (¾ inch) thick, on a baking tray lined with greaseproof paper. Place in the oven at the lowest temperature setting and leave for about 6–7 hours until dry and brittle.
3 Put half of the strawberries into a blender with half of the sugar and whiz until smooth, then pass through a sieve to remove the seeds.
4 Whisk the double cream, remaining caster sugar and vanilla extract together in a bowl until stiff. Break the meringue into small pieces and fold into the cream with half of the strawberry purée. Don't mix it together too thoroughly; you want a ripple effect.
5 Slice the remaining strawberries. Spoon the cream mixture into the middle of each serving plate, then spoon most of the strawberry purée over and around the outside. Scatter the sliced strawberries on top and drizzle with the remaining strawberry purée to serve.

This summer dessert is so easy, especially if you make the meringue in advance, or cheat by buying about 125g (4oz) good quality ready-made meringue. Try it with different berries during the summer months.

Summer pudding

Illustrated on previous pages

Serves 4

900g (2lb) mixed summer fruits,
   such as strawberries (hulled and
   halved), raspberries, redcurrants,
   blueberries and blackberries
150g (5oz) caster sugar
about ½ large loaf good quality white
   bread

1 Put all the fruits and sugar into a saucepan, bring to a simmer and cook for 2 minutes to soften the fruit slightly, then leave to cool a little. (If using frozen fruit, drain off any juices after defrosting, then combine with the sugar, bring to a simmer and immediately remove from the heat.) Whiz about one sixth of the fruit and juice in a blender until smooth and set to one side to serve with the pudding.

2 Cut the bread into 5–8mm (¼–⅜ inch) thick slices and remove the crusts. Line a 1 litre (1¾ pint) pudding basin with cling film, allowing it to overhang the sides. Cut a circle from one slice of bread to fit the base. Cut the rest of the bread into pieces to fit around the sides and extend slightly above the rim, overlapping them slightly and pressing the joins together with your fingers.

3 Spoon the fruit and a little of the juice into the lined basin to come halfway up. Cover with a round of bread, then top up with the rest of the fruit and juice. Cut some more bread to fit the top and position, then fold the bread around the side over it a little. Bring the cling film up over the pudding and twist to seal. Cover with a plate and place a couple of cans (or something else heavy) on top to weight it down. Leave overnight in the fridge.

4 To serve, run a knife around the pudding to loosen it, hold a plate upside down on top and invert to turn out. Spoon the reserved fruit sauce over the pudding and serve, with some thick Jersey cream.

This is a good way to use a glut of summer fruit, though it also works well with frozen mixed fruits. Avoid a high proportion of tart fruits like blackcurrants, or the flavour will be too sour. Use individual pudding basins to make single portion puddings if you prefer.

Autumn fruits in mulled wine

Serves 4

200ml (7fl oz) full-bodied fruity red
  wine (like a New World Merlot)
1 small cinnamon stick
4 cloves
1 bay leaf
200g (7oz) brown sugar
few strips of orange peel
4 ripe plums
2 ripe pears
200g (7oz) blackberries, elderberries
  or blueberries

1 Put the red wine into a pan with the cinnamon, cloves, bay leaf, sugar and orange peel. Bring to the boil and simmer gently for 5 minutes. Remove from the heat and leave to cool.

2 Meanwhile, quarter and stone the plums. Peel, halve and core the pears, then cut each half into 6 wedges. Put all the fruits into a bowl and pour the mulled wine over them. Cover and leave for at least 2 hours, stirring occasionally. Serve at room temperature, with thick Jersey cream.

This very simple dessert makes good use of blackberries that are a little tart to eat on their own. Try using other fruits instead of pears and plums, such as apples and greengages.

Pear and blackberry crumble

Serves 4
6 large ripe pears
25g (1oz) unsalted butter
100g (3½oz) fresh or frozen
  blackberries
50–65g (2–2½oz) caster sugar

For the crumble topping
75g (3oz) unsalted butter, diced
40g (1½oz) ground almonds
125g (4oz) caster sugar
160g (5½oz) plain flour

1 Preheat the oven to 180°C (fan oven 160°C), gas mark 4. Peel, core and roughly chop the pears. Melt the butter in a pan, add the pears and cook over a high heat, turning frequently, until soft and most of the liquid has evaporated. Add the blackberries and sugar to taste, stir until the sugar is dissolved and take off the heat.

2 To make the crumble topping, mix all the ingredients in a food processor or mixer, or place in a bowl and rub together using your fingertips, until the mixture resembles breadcrumbs.

3 Fill a baking dish with the pear mixture and spoon the crumble evenly over the top. Bake for 20–30 minutes until the topping is golden brown. Serve with clotted cream or custard (see page 252).

Crumbles are usually associated with apples and rhubarb, but you can easily vary the fruit. Add some dried fruits in winter and scatter in berry fruits during the summer. The topping can also be jazzed up by adding oats or nuts.

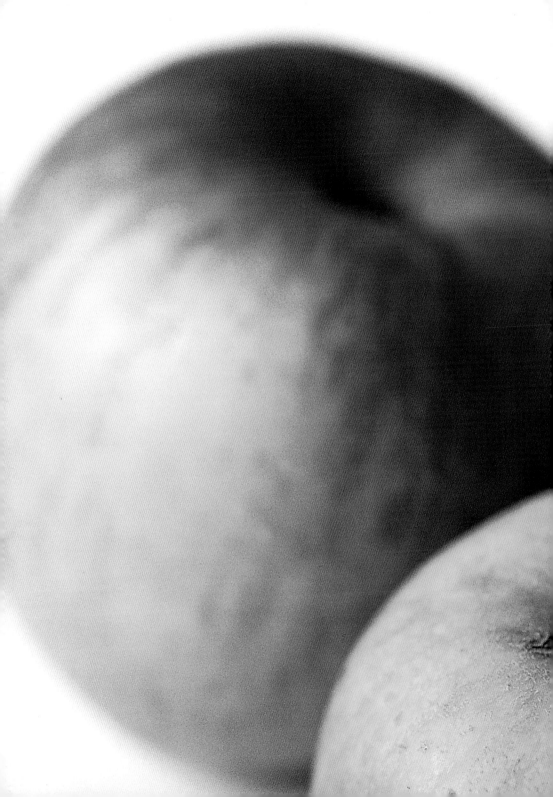

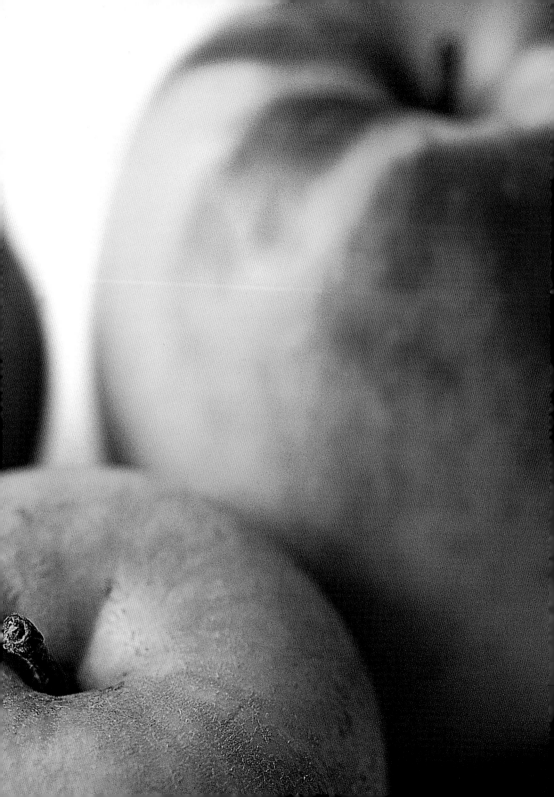

Baked apples and custard

Serves 4

4 large apples, such as Cox's Orange
    Pippins, Braeburn or Jonagold
8 tbsp luxury mincemeat
65g (2½oz) fresh white breadcrumbs
1 tsp ground cinnamon
2 tbsp brown sugar

For the custard

300ml (½ pint) single cream
½ vanilla pod, split lengthways
5 medium egg yolks
65g (2½oz) caster sugar
2 tsp cornflour

1 Preheat the oven to 190°C (fan oven 170°C), gas mark 5. Using an apple
corer, scoop out the cores from the apples. Mix the mincemeat, breadcrumbs,
cinnamon and sugar together. Put each apple on a larger piece of foil and fill
the core cavities with the mincemeat mixture. Fold the foil up loosely around
each apple and stand them on a baking tray.

2 Bake the apples in the oven for 45–60 minutes or until they are soft. Check
them individually after 40 minutes, as the odd one may need removing
before the rest if it cooks more quickly.

3 Meanwhile, make the custard. Put the cream in a small pan. Scrape the
seeds from the vanilla pod into the cream and add the empty pod. Bring to
the boil, take off the heat and leave to infuse for 10 minutes, then remove
the pod. Whisk the egg yolks with the sugar and cornflour, then pour on the
cream, whisking all the time. Return to the pan. Cook gently over a low heat
for a few minutes, stirring constantly with a wooden spoon until the custard
thickens; don't let it boil or it may curdle.

4 Serve the baked apples with the custard.

Apples can react differently during cooking –
you may find that one takes more or less time
than the rest. The filling can be varied to taste
with more or less spice, or the addition of nuts
like ground almonds or walnuts.

Sussex pond pudding

Serves 4–6
250g (9oz) self-raising flour, plus
  extra to dust
125g (4oz) shredded beef suet
150ml (¼ pint) milk

300g (11oz) unsalted butter,
  softened, plus extra to grease
200g (7oz) soft light brown sugar
1 large unwaxed lemon

1 Mix the flour and suet together in a bowl, then gradually mix in the milk
to form a dough. The dough should be soft but firm enough to roll out.
2 Roll out the dough to a circle large enough to line a 1.5 litre (2½ pint)
pudding basin. Cut a quarter out of the circle for the lid and to ease the
lining of the bowl. Butter the pudding basin well, drop the pastry into it and
join up the edges where the quarter was removed.
3 Mix the butter and sugar together and put into the lined basin. With a
roasting fork or skewer, prick the whole lemon all over and thoroughly so
the juices can escape during cooking, then push it into the butter mixture.
4 Remould the pastry for the top and roll it out to the correct size. Lay it on
top of the filling and press the edges together to seal in the filling. Cover the
top of the basin with a generous piece of foil, making a pleat down the
middle to allow for expansion. Secure in place under the rim with string,
making a string handle so it can be lifted out easily.
5 Lower the pudding into a pan containing enough boiling water to come
about halfway up the side of the basin. Cover and simmer for 4 hours,
topping up with more boiling water as necessary.
6 To serve, lift out the basin and allow to stand for about 30 minutes, then
remove the foil and loosen the sides with a small sharp knife. Put a deep
serving dish over the basin and quickly turn the whole thing upside down –
it may collapse a little but the flavour will be incredible.

This unusual pudding is steamed with a whole
lemon inside, which permeates the buttery
sauce with its flavour as it cooks. When the
pudding is turned out, it will be sitting in a
pond of sweet lemony sauce.

Spotted dick

Illustrated on previous pages

Serves 4–6
360g (12½oz) plain flour
pinch of salt
2 tsp baking powder
180g (6¼oz) suet
125g (4oz) soft brown sugar
175g (6oz) currants
grated zest of 1 lemon
½ tsp ground mixed spice
about 150ml (¼ pint) milk
butter, to grease and serve
golden syrup, to serve

1 Sift the flour, salt and baking powder together into a large mixing bowl.
Stir in the suet, sugar, currants, lemon zest and mixed spice, then add just
enough milk to make a soft dough.
2 Shape the dough into a log shape and wrap loosely in a sheet of buttered
heavy-duty cling film. Wrap this loosely in muslin and secure with string.
Drop into a large pan of boiling water and simmer for 2 hours. If using a
cylindrical mould, line it with buttered greaseproof paper, put the dough in
the mould and steam for 2½ hours.
3 To serve, remove the wrappings and cut the pudding into 3cm (1¼ inch)
slices. Serve with a knob of butter and drizzle with golden syrup.

This is one of the most popular comfort puddings from school days. It can be served with custard, or even more simply with golden syrup and a knob of butter. Spotted dick is one of the honoured members of the roly poly family and should be steamed. You can even buy cylindrical moulds for the purpose.

Sticky toffee pudding

Serves 4–6

150g (5oz) pitted dates

65g (2½oz) unsalted butter, plus
   extra to grease

175g (6oz) soft dark brown sugar

2 medium eggs, lightly beaten

225g (8oz) self-raising flour

For the toffee sauce

600ml (1 pint) double cream

350g (12oz) caster sugar

90g (3¼oz) unsalted butter

1 Put the dates into a pan with 250ml (8fl oz) water and simmer over a low heat for 10–15 minutes or until the dates are soft and the water has almost evaporated. Whiz in a blender until smooth. The purée should be a good spoonable consistency; if too thick, thin with a little water. Leave to cool.

2 Preheat the oven to 180°C (fan oven 160°C), gas mark 4. Soften the butter. Grease a baking tin, measuring about 15 x 12 x 6cm (6 x 5 x 2½ inches), with butter and line with greaseproof paper.

3 To make the sponge, in a food processor, mixer or by hand, cream the butter and sugar together until light and fluffy. Add the eggs slowly, taking care that the mixture does not separate. (If this happens, add a little of the flour and continue mixing for a minute or so.) Then gently fold in the flour, with a large metal spoon, until evenly mixed. Finally, fold in the date purée.

4 Spread the mixture in the baking tin and bake for about 50–60 minutes or until the sponge is firm to the touch. Allow to cool in the tin for 10 minutes or so. Keep the oven on.

5 Meanwhile, make the toffee sauce. Pour half of the cream into a heavy-based pan and add the sugar and butter. Bring to the boil, stirring, and continue to boil for 8–10 minutes or even longer until the sauce is golden brown. Allow the sauce to cool for about 10 minutes, then whisk in the remaining cream.

6 Remove the sponge from the tin, trim the edges to neaten, then cut horizontally into 4 even layers. Re-line the tin with fresh greaseproof paper. Re-assemble the sponge in the tin, spreading two thirds of the warm sauce in between the layers. Reheat the pudding in the oven for 15–20 minutes.

7 To serve, cut the pudding into 4 to 6 portions, place in warm bowls and top with the remaining toffee sauce. Serve with ice cream, soured cream or crème fraîche.

Apple charlotte

Serves 4

1.5kg (3¼lb) Bramleys or other good
   cooking apples
140g (4½oz) unsalted butter
about 100g (3½oz) caster sugar,
   depending on sweetness of apples
10–14 thin slices of good quality
   white bread or brioche

1 Peel, quarter and core the apples, then cut into chunks. Melt 50g (2oz) of the butter in a heavy-based saucepan. Add the apples and sugar, cover and cook over a medium heat, stirring occasionally, for 8–10 minutes or so until softened. Remove the lid and cook until the liquid has evaporated and the apples are quite dry and cooked through but not puréed.

2 Preheat the oven to 200°C (fan oven 180°C), gas mark 6. Have ready 4 individual metal or foil pudding basins, measuring 8–9cm (3¼–3½ inches) across and 5–6cm (2–2½ inches) deep. Remove the crusts from the bread and melt the rest of the butter.

3 From each of 8 bread slices, cut a disc slightly smaller than the top of the pudding basins. Then cut 8 rectangular pieces of bread, about 7 x 12cm (2¾ x 5 inches), from the other slices. These will line the walls of the basin, so the shorter side of the bread should be the same as the depth of the pudding basins, and 2 slices wrapped around the inside of the pudding basin should overlap slightly.

4 To make the casing for the puddings, dip both sides of the bread rectangles in the melted butter and line the sides of each mould with two rectangular pieces, overlapping them slightly at the two joints. Dip the discs of bread into the butter on both sides and push one into the bottom of each mould with your fingers to fit snugly; make sure there aren't any gaps. Fill the moulds with the apple mixture. Top each with the 4 remaining bread discs, again dipped in butter, and pinch the edges of the bread together with your fingers to seal.

5 Cover the tops of the puddings loosely with foil and bake for 15 minutes. Turn the oven down to 170°C (fan oven 150°C), gas mark 3 and cook for a further 20 minutes. Turn each charlotte upside down on to a serving plate and leave covered with the mould for up to 20 minutes until ready to serve. Remove the moulds and serve the charlottes with thick pouring cream.

Rice pudding with vanilla apricot compote

Serves 4

100g (3½oz) pudding rice
50g (2oz) caster sugar
pinch of freshly grated nutmeg
600ml (1 pint) full-fat milk
100ml (3½fl oz) double cream
150ml (¼ pint) evaporated milk

For the vanilla apricot compote

½ vanilla pod
25g (1oz) unsalted butter
25g (1oz) caster sugar
12 ripe apricots, halved and stoned

1 Put the rice, caster sugar, nutmeg and full-fat milk into a pan and bring to the boil, then lower the heat and simmer for 20 minutes or until the rice is tender, stirring from time to time.

2 Add the cream and evaporated milk, bring back a simmer and cook gently for another 10 minutes. Remove from the heat. If you are serving the rice pudding cold, set aside to cool.

3 To make the apricot compote, split the vanilla pod in half lengthways and scrape out the seeds with the tip of a knife. Put the butter and sugar into a saucepan with the vanilla and 1 tbsp water. Simmer for about 5 minutes until the sugar has melted and the mixture has thickened. Add the apricots, cover with a lid and cook for 10 minutes. Remove from the heat and set aside to cool if required.

4 Serve the rice pudding with the apricot compote, either hot or cold.

Rice pudding is given a sophisticated twist with this compote, but you could just serve it with good old jam. Ready-to-eat dried apricots, soaked overnight in warm water, can be used for the compote if fresh ones are out of season.

The classic British cheeseboard

These days a little cheese is sometimes served before dessert, as opposed to after it, or even in some cases instead of it. I personally don't mind either way, though a plate of cheese on the dinner table after dessert can sometimes be a good way to finish up the red wine. In France, of course, cheese after dessert is unheard of, so there is no choice in the matter.

Cheese-makers in the British Isles are now making some amazing cheeses, and always have, but until recently there hasn't been the commercial demand for them and restaurants have tended to offer a 'French-only' cheeseboard, with maybe a token Stilton. I remember, as a child, hearing about Blue Vinney and how difficult it was to get hold of. Now, of course, it sits on supermarket shelves alongside other well-made English blues, like Jersey and Yorkshire blue. The array of English goat's cheeses now available includes fresh creamy ones and hard matured cheeses that match up to any in the world.

The Irish seem to have grasped the whole business of cheesemaking and I would happily sit confronted with a plate of Duras, Coleeney and Cashel Blue, among others. Cheeses of the British Isles should be of top eating quality, because we have such good dairy products and first-class milk with which to produce them.

Salad doesn't complement our semi-hard to hard cheeses in the same way it does the soft French cheeses. Chutneys and pickles are our pièces de resistance, and crisp celery doesn't go amiss. Recently I have started to complement cheeses with jellies. My homemade blackcurrant jelly is the perfect match for Stilton and similar British blue cheeses, like Harbourne Blue and Yorkshire Blue, or the French Roquefort. Alternatively, you can always buy a pot of good-quality port jelly to serve with the Stilton and other cheeses at Christmas.

Blackcurrant jelly

Place 450g (1lb) blackcurrants (or blackberries) and 450g (1lb) caster sugar sugar in a large heavy-based saucepan and gently bring to the boil, stirring. Skim off any scum that rises to the surface and simmer for 1 hour. Pass through a fine sieve, pour into two sterilised 450g (1lb) jars and leave to set. Store in the fridge for up to 2 months.

british
teatime

Cucumber sandwiches

Makes 4 rounds

½ cucumber

8 slices of wholemeal or light
   caraway bread

good butter or cream cheese, for
   spreading

sea salt and pepper

1 Halve, deseed and thinly slice the cucumber, but don't peel it. Scatter the slices on a tray, season lightly with fine sea salt and leave for 10 minutes. As the salt draws moisture out, so it concentrates the flavour of the cucumber. Pat the slices dry with kitchen paper.

2 Season the cucumber with black pepper. Spread the slices of bread with butter or a little cream cheese if you prefer (though the cucumber flavour is sufficient without). Sandwich the cucumber slices between the bread slices and serve.

Cucumber and salmon sandwiches: For a more substantial sandwich, mix some flaked hot-smoked salmon, freshly poached salmon or cooked white crabmeat with a little good quality mayonnaise, a squeeze of lemon juice and a little chopped dill. Sandwich the bread slices together with this mixture and the cucumber slices.

Cucumber sandwiches are classic afternoon tea fare, first served with tea when it became a fashionable drink in the early 1800s. Freshly baked bread is a good starting point and naturally, good farmhouse butter.

Egg mayonnaise sandwiches

Makes 4 rounds

4 eggs
2 tbsp good quality mayonnaise,
    preferably homemade (see page 56)
a little English mustard (optional)
8 slices of wholemeal or Granary
    bread
few watercress leaves, chopped
    (optional)
sea salt and pepper

1 Cook the eggs in a pan of simmering water for about 4 minutes, so that the yolk is just cooked. Drain and cool under cold running water, until they are cool enough to shell.
2 Spike the mayonnaise with a little English mustard if you like. Chop your eggs, fold in the mayonnaise and season with salt and pepper to taste.
3 Sandwich between slices of wholemeal or Granary bread and add a few chopped watercress leaves, if you wish.

Watercress sandwiches: Watercress has an amazing freshness with a little kick of heat, which makes it perfect between two slices of bread. Pile rinsed and dried watercress sprigs thickly between buttered slices of good white or brown bread, with a little sea salt for the perfect sandwich.

Afternoon tea, with its delicate sandwiches followed by selections of cakes and pastries, is an old English tradition, famously served at hotels such as the Ritz, and popular in country teahouses, thatched inns and seaside cafes.

Scones

Makes 12

225g (8oz) plain flour, plus extra to
dust
2 tsp baking powder
50g (2oz) butter, cut into small
pieces
pinch of salt
1 tsp sugar
about 150ml (¼ pint) milk

To serve

clotted cream
strawberry or other jam (preferably
homemade)

1 Preheat the oven to 220°C (fan oven 200°C), gas mark 7. Sift the flour and
baking powder together into a mixing bowl, then rub in the butter until the
mixture has the texture of breadcrumbs. Stir in the salt and sugar, then
slowly mix in just enough milk to form a stiff dough.

2 Gently pat or roll out the dough on a lightly floured surface to a 1.5–2cm
(⅝–¾ inch) thickness. Cut out rounds, using a 6–7cm (2½–2¾ inch) plain
cutter. Arrange well apart on a baking sheet and bake for 10–15 minutes
until well risen and golden.

3 Transfer the cooked scones to a wire rack and allow to cool slightly. Serve
them warm, with clotted cream and jam.

Served with clotted cream and strawberry jam,
scones are at the heart of a West Country
cream tea. They are always best eaten on the
day they are made, though they can be frozen
and warmed through.

Drop scones

Also illustrated on previous pages

Makes 8–12
225g (8oz) plain flour
½ tsp bicarbonate of soda
½ tsp cream of tartar
50g (2oz) granulated sugar
2 medium eggs, beaten
about 275ml (9fl oz) milk
a little oil, to oil pan

To serve
fruit compote or fresh berries and
  cream, or soft butter

1 Sift the flour, bicarbonate of soda and cream of tartar into a large mixing bowl, then add the sugar. Stir in the eggs and enough of the milk to form a smooth batter.
2 Heat a griddle pan or non-stick frying pan and oil it lightly. Drop spoonfuls of the mixture into the pan, spacing them well apart to allow for expansion. Let them cook for 3 minutes until bubbles rise to the surface, then turn the scones over and cook for another 2–3 minutes. Remove and place on some kitchen paper to drain. Keep warm while you cook the rest, wiping the pan and oiling again for each batch.
3 Serve the drop scones warm, with fruit compote or fresh berries and cream, or just some butter.

Also called Scotch pancakes, these scones are aptly named because the mixture is dropped from the spoon directly on to the griddle. They are delicious served warm with butter, or topped with a spoonful of berry compote.

Shortbread

Makes about 8–12 pieces

480g (1lb 1oz) plain flour, plus extra
    to dust
125g (4oz) caster sugar, plus extra
    to dust
360g (12½oz) unsalted butter, cut
    into small pieces
2 medium eggs, beaten

1 Mix the flour and sugar together in a bowl, then rub in the butter with your fingertips until the mixture resembles breadcrumbs. Make a well in the centre and add the beaten eggs. Mix well to form a smooth dough.

2 Transfer the dough to a lightly floured surface. Roll out to a thickness of about 5mm (¼ inch) or a little thicker if you wish, in a round or rectangle (depending on the shape required). Mark into wedges or fingers and prick all over with a fork.

3 Transfer the shortbread to a baking tray and chill for about 30 minutes. Meanwhile, preheat the oven to 180°C (fan oven 160°C), gas mark 4. Bake the shortbread for 15–20 minutes or until lightly coloured. Dust with caster sugar while still warm. Store in an airtight container until required.

Originally from Scotland, shortbread has lots of variations, from the addition of rice flour in some parts of Scotland to demerara sugar in Dorset, and caraway and coriander in the similar Goosnargh cakes of Lancashire.

Eccles cakes

Illustrated on previous pages

Makes 12–15
225g (8oz) plain flour, plus extra to
  dust
pinch of salt
90g (3¼oz) butter, frozen
90g (3¼oz) lard, frozen

For the filling
75g (3oz) butter
150g (5oz) soft brown sugar
150g (5oz) currants
1 tsp ground cinnamon
½ tsp freshly grated nutmeg
grated zest of 1 orange
50g (2oz) chopped mixed candied
  peel
To glaze
2 medium egg whites
caster sugar, to sprinkle

1 To make the pastry, sift the flour and salt into a bowl, then coarsely grate the frozen butter and lard over the flour. Distribute the fats evenly through the flour, using a metal spoon. Add just enough cold water to form a pliable dough, then wrap in cling film and refrigerate for 30 minutes.
2 Meanwhile, make the filling. Melt the butter in a pan and mix it with all the other ingredients. Preheat the oven to 220°C (fan oven 200°C), gas mark 7.
3 Roll the pastry out on a floured surface to a 3mm (⅛ inch) thickness. Cut out rounds, using a plain 9cm (3½ inch) cutter. Put a heaped teaspoonful of filling in the centre of each round and brush the edge of half the circle with a little water. Draw the edges up over the filling and pinch together to resemble an old-fashioned purse.
4 Turn the 'purses' over, then gently flatten with a rolling pin and cut a slit in the top of each one. Brush with egg white, sprinkle with caster sugar and bake for 15 minutes. Serve just warm.

Named after the small town on the outskirts of Manchester where they were first made, eccles cakes are delicious eaten on their own, or with a hard cheese, like Lancashire. They are traditionally made with flaky pastry, as here, but puff pastry is an alternative.

Hot cross buns

Illustrated on previous pages

Makes 20

650g (1lb 7oz) strong plain flour,
 plus extra to dust
1 tsp ground cinnamon
1 tsp freshly grated nutmeg
1 tsp ground mixed spice
½ tsp ground mace
½ tsp salt
65g (2½oz) caster sugar
90g (3¼oz) butter
7g (¼oz) sachet fast-action dried
 yeast
200ml (7fl oz) warm milk
200ml (7fl oz) hot water
1 medium egg, beaten
100g (3½oz) raisins
65g (2½oz) chopped mixed candied
 peel

To finish

1 medium egg, beaten
40g (1½oz) plain flour
few drops of almond extract
65g (2½oz) caster sugar
6 cubes of white sugar, coarsely
 crushed

1 Sift the flour, spices and salt into a warm mixing bowl and stir in the sugar. Rub in the butter and stir in the dried yeast. Add the warm milk, hot water and egg, and mix to a soft dough.

2 Knead the dough by stretching and folding it for about 10 minutes on a lightly floured surface.

3 Knead the raisins and mixed peel into the dough, then roll the dough into a long sausage shape. Cut into 20 discs with a knife, then shape these into buns. Place them, at least 5cm (2 inches) apart, on a baking tray lined with greaseproof paper. Cover with cling film and leave to prove in a warm place for 30 minutes. Preheat the oven to 230°C (fan oven 210°C), gas mark 8.

4 Remove the cling film and brush the buns with the beaten egg. Mix the flour to a paste with a little water and the almond extract. Put into a piping bag and pipe a wide cross on top of each bun.

5 Bake the buns for 15 minutes, then transfer to a rack to cool. While they are still warm, mix the caster sugar and crushed sugar cubes with 5 tbsp water. Brush the buns with this mixture and leave to cool.

To enjoy hot cross buns at their best, serve them warm, split and buttered.

Dundee cake

Makes an 18cm (7 inch) cake

150g (5oz) unsalted butter, softened
  at room temperature, plus extra
  to grease

150g (5oz) caster sugar

3 medium eggs, beaten

225g (8oz) plain flour

1 tsp baking powder

175g (6oz) currants

175g (6oz) sultanas

50g (2oz) glacé cherries, rinsed,
  dried and halved

50g (2oz) mixed candied peel, finely
  chopped

2 tbsp ground almonds

finely grated zest of 1 lemon

finely grated zest of 1 orange

For the topping

about 25g (1oz) whole blanched
  almonds

1 Preheat the oven to 170ºC (fan oven 150ºC), gas mark 3. Lightly grease a deep 18–20cm (7–8 inch) round cake tin, then line the base and sides with greaseproof paper.

2 In a mixing bowl using a wooden spoon or electric mixer, cream the butter and sugar together until you get a pale mixture that drops off a spoon easily. Add the eggs a little at a time, beating the mixture thoroughly after each addition.

3 Sift the flour and baking powder together. Add this to the cake mixture in 4 stages, each time gently folding it in with a large metal spoon to keep the mixture light. Again, when the flour is all incorporated, the mixture should drop off a spoon easily.

4 Gently fold in the rest of the ingredients, except for the whole almonds, and spoon the mixture into the cake tin, spreading it evenly with the back of a spoon. Carefully arrange the whole almonds on the top in a circle; do not press them in though, or they will sink during baking.

5 Bake the cake on the middle shelf of the oven for 2–2½ hours or until it looks firm and the top feels springy to the touch. If the cake appears to be browning too quickly during cooking, cover the top loosely with foil. To test, insert a thin skewer into the middle; it should come out clean.

6 Leave the cake to cool in the tin for about 15 minutes, then run a knife around the edge to loosen it and remove. Place on a wire rack and leave to cool completely.

7 When cold, wrap the cake in greaseproof paper and transfer to an airtight container. Dundee cake is best allowed to mature for a couple of days or so before cutting.

This is a lighter recipe than those heavy fruit cakes that tend to get left at Christmas time. Apparently, Dundee cake was created by Keillers, the famous marmalade makers of Dundee, to use up excess citrus rind that wasn't needed for marmalade.

Madeira cake

Makes a 20cm (8 inch) cake
175g (6oz) butter, at room
    temperature, plus extra to grease
175g (6oz) caster sugar
4 medium eggs, beaten
grated zest of ½ lemon
275g (10oz) plain flour
½ tsp baking powder

1 Preheat the oven to 180°C (fan oven 160°C), gas mark 4 and line a 20cm
(8 inch) cake tin with buttered greaseproof paper.
2 In a mixing bowl, with a wooden spoon or electric mixer, cream the butter
and sugar together until you get a pale mixture that drops off a spoon
easily. Add the eggs a little at a time, beating the mixture thoroughly after
each addition. Stir in the grated lemon zest.
3 Sift the flour and baking powder together and add it to the mixture in
4 stages, each time gently folding it in with a metal spoon to keep the
mixture light.
4 Spoon the mixture into the prepared cake tin and bake for 1½ hours. Leave
in the tin for 10 minutes or so, then turn out and cool on a wire rack.

This 19th-century cake was traditionally
served with a glass of Madeira, hence the
name. It's less fashionable now, but still a
good, simple teatime cake.

Banana bread

Makes about 20 slices

90g (3¼oz) butter, melted, plus extra
    to grease
240g (8½oz) plain flour
1 tsp salt
1 tsp baking powder
1 tsp ground cinnamon
125g (4oz) caster sugar
1 medium egg, beaten
few drops of vanilla extract
100g (3½oz) pecan nuts, chopped
4 ripe bananas, peeled and mashed

1 Preheat the oven to 190°C (fan oven 170°C), gas mark 5 and lightly grease
a 900g (2lb) loaf tin.
2 Sift the flour, salt, baking powder and cinnamon into a mixing bowl and
stir in the sugar. Gently mix in the egg, butter and vanilla, then fold in the
nuts and bananas.
3 Turn the mixture into the loaf tin and bake for 40–50 minutes until a
skewer inserted in the centre comes out dry. Leave in the tin for 10 minutes
before turning out on a wire rack to cool completely.

The bananas ensure that this teabread stays
nice and moist for a few days. It is delicious
served just as it is, or topped with jam.

Lardy cake

Makes about 12 squares

650g (1lb 7oz) strong white bread
flour, plus extra to dust

2 tsp salt

1 tsp caster sugar, plus extra to
sprinkle

7g (¼oz) sachet fast-action dried
yeast

200g (7oz) lard, softened

50g (2oz) butter, softened

200g (7oz) mixed dried fruit

75g (3oz) chopped mixed candied
peel

200g (7oz) granulated sugar

1 In a warm mixing bowl, mix the flour, salt, sugar and yeast together and make a well in the middle. Add 400ml (14fl oz) warm water and mix to a smooth, soft dough.

2 Turn on to a lightly floured surface and knead the dough by stretching and folding it for about 10 minutes.

3 Mix the lard, butter, fruit, peel and granulated sugar together and divide into 3 portions.

4 On a lightly floured surface, roll out the bread dough to a rectangle, roughly three times as long as it is wide. Spread two thirds of its length with one batch of the lard mixture, then fold both long ends of the dough into the centre and firmly press the edges with your fingers or the rolling pin. Repeat this process twice more, using up the lard mixture.

5 Put the dough into a shallow baking tin with enough room for it to rise. Leave to prove in a warm place for about 30 minutes. Meanwhile, preheat the oven to 190°C (fan oven 170°C), gas mark 5.

6 Bake the lardy cake in the oven for about 45 minutes. Turn it out upside down on to another tray or large dish and allow to cool a little. Sprinkle the cake generously with caster sugar. Serve while still warm, cut into generous squares.

The amount of lard, sugar and fruit in this traditional pastry varies in different recipes from around the country, and you can put in more or less, depending on your taste. It is essential, though, to serve lardy cake slightly warm, ideally still fresh from the oven.

Index